The Complete Complainer

How to Complain and Get Results

JASPER GRIEGSON

metro

First published in Great Britain in 2000 by Metro Books (an imprint of Metro Publishing Limited), 19 Gerrard Street, London W1V 7LA

Any views or opinions are solely those of the author and do not necessarily represent those of Express Newspapers.

British Library Cataloguing in Publication Data. A CIP record of this book is available on request from the British Library.
ISBN 1 900512 86 6

10 9 8 7 6 5 4 3 2 1

Typeset by Wakewing, High Wycombe, Buckinghamshire
Printed in Britain by Omnia Books Limited, Glasgow

The Complete
Complainer

THE EXPRESS

Jasper Griegson's column 'The Complainer' appears every Saturday in the *Express*

CONTENTS

Introduction

The British are a strange breed. We are defeatists. It is only when faced with invasion that we decide to put our boxing gloves on. The rest of the time we mill around, bemoaning our lack of sporting prowess, criticising the weather and ranting about the government's latest economic bungle. We mutter and we moan but on the whole we despair.

This defect in the British make-up is the reason why our trains grind to a halt at the sight of a few brown leaves, our shop assistants chew gum and look gormless when asked a simple question and our hairdryers fall to bits one day after the expiry of the guarantee. We get what we deserve and what we deserve is bad service and shoddy goods. Why? Because we don't complain enough.

This book is not designed to turn you into a moaning minnie because complaining and moaning are two very distinct concepts. Moaning means sitting slumped back in your armchair and doing nothing to change whatever is troubling you. Complaining means sitting at a desk with a piece of paper and taking positive and decisive steps to rectify whatever has gone wrong. Moaning is free. Although by contrast it is not free, complaining costs no more than the price of a postage stamp.

There is an easy way out when you have bought a settee that collapses when you sit on it, or when your holiday in Marbella resembles a prison sentence. You are perfectly at liberty to do nothing. You can even adopt the moral high ground by refusing to complain on the basis that you are not a Victor Meldrew. Unfortunately Victor has given complaining a very bad name since, as a result of his extremely funny ranting, complaining has become inextricably associated with madness, senility and misery. In truth the soft option is the worst option because doing nothing leaves you unhappy, outraged and without a settee.

The reason why most people hate to complain is because complaining 'isn't cricket'. Complaining is about being non-defeatist and assertive. It's about winning. It goes against the grain to adopt a non-stiff-upper-lip approach to adversity. Once you have overcome this deep-seated psychological hurdle, anything is possible.

If you have never written a letter of complaint in your life but your brand-new Ford Mondeo has been sent back to the garage for the fifth time in as many months, the best starting point is as follows. Pour yourself (a) a piping-hot bath and (b) enough stiff gin to give yourself a hefty dose of Dutch courage. When you are lying in the bath imagine a similar bath somewhere else in Britain. In that bath picture the Managing Director of Ford UK gently scrubbing his or her back with a loofah. For the princely sum of 27p you can communicate with that person or, at the very least, you can try. That other person is not a monster with fangs, green saliva and cloven hooves. He or she is not the devil incarnate but rather an ordinary human being who, quite probably, would be horrified to learn how badly you have been treated by the staff at your local Ford dealer. Overcome the fear of communication and you are half-way to solving the problem.

The next mental step requires you to disassociate the process of writing from what you used to do at school. Writing a letter of complaint is not the same as writing a ten-page discourse about what you did during the summer holidays. A letter of complaint should be short, concise and crystal-clear. A rambling essay is not required and no one is going to make you write it again just because the grammar is below par.

If you make it to the stage of putting pen to paper (although for clarity's sake a typed letter is infinitely preferable) the battle is almost won. Limit your letter to one page and, striking while the iron is hot, post it immediately. Even if it does not ultimately lead to a replacement car or a life-long supply of chocolate buttons, the mere catharsis of complaining will make you feel better about yourself.

Your letter should be addressed by name to someone at the top of the organisation concerned and, without being abusive or emotional, it should convey (a) the nature of the problem; (b) your extreme disappointment; and (c) a demand for action or compensation. You should attach to it copies of any relevant paperwork such as invoices, receipts or guarantees. It is essential that you retain a copy of whatever you send and keep it safe for round two of the battle.

Although you may, in true Lennox Lewis style, achieve a knockout victory with one letter, you may have to slug it out longer. You may receive a flippant reply from Customer Services or a paltry offer of a few worthless tokens. It is a good idea to make a pre-emptive strike in your opening letter by finishing with a salvo of the following kind: 'Let me assure you now that a dismissive two-line apology from your Customer Services Department will not satisfy me'. Insurance companies are the worst offenders in this respect. The first letter will always tell you to go to hell (in the nicest possible way) because they know full well that at least 25 per cent of people give up at that point.

If necessary, you may have to dig in for the winter and fight a much longer campaign. If the problem is big enough and your resolve strong enough, it may take a protracted war to succeed.

Thereafter, even if you hate the game or don't know how to play it, you should treat your complaint as akin to a chess match. You may need to outwit your opponent, you may need to devise a cunning strategy or you may need to make a minor concession in order to achieve ultimate victory. Above all else you should adopt a positively Churchillian approach to the battle. Do not be defeated by ill-informed, indifferent counter staff, idiotic customer services staff, computer-generated correspondence or your own apathy. The more you apply yourself to making yourself heard, the more you are likely to enjoy the very process of expressing yourself. Therein lies the trick. If you make the psychological switch from moaning mode to complaining mode, you will discover that consumer assertiveness is great fun. Subject to the laws of defamation, you can write whatever you like to whomever you like and in a style that suits you. The more flamboyant complainer will venture into poetry, medieval script or descriptive drawings. The more subdued complainer will adhere to a conservative format. It matters not. The key to complaining is to do it. You should not pretend that the problem doesn't exist nor should you pay lip service to the idea of complaining and then allow a solution to wither on the vine. Whenever you encounter a problem, hit it on the head with a powerful missive to a senior executive and results will follow as night follows day.

Very often, the reason why complaints are not dealt with properly is not the fault of the company concerned. Companies actually like complaints because complaints supply them with valuable feedback that otherwise they would only get by paying for it. Reputable companies want to hear about your problem, because they want to retain you as a loyal customer. In order for them to do this you need to communicate your complaint in a clear and effective way. Complaints are like lorries – they need to be articulated. You do not need to be a journalist or an English professor to write a letter. As long as you can write, you can complain. A moaner is comparable to a crying baby. A distressed baby cannot express itself other than by letting out a primeval scream. It is very hard to tell from a scream whether the baby wants a Marmite sandwich or its nappy changed. It is similarly difficult for a company to understand its weaknesses and faults when its aggrieved customers either (a) do nothing at all or (b) march up to the returns desk, start swearing and then head-butt the 19-year-old customer-services trainee. To complain is to graduate from wailing to communicating.

Why should you complain? The results and the catharsis are enough to motivate me, but there is, on a higher plane, a more important reason to complain. Complaining is a bit like voting. By complaining you are exercising an important democratic right. If something is wrong you should let your voice be heard, if only to put it right for the benefit of future users. If the toilets at your favourite local fast-food chain are disgustingly dirty you should tell the powers that be. Your initial vile encounter with dirty sinks and shredded hand towels cannot be undone but you genuinely possess the power to change the situation. A three-line letter from you and a couple of other aggrieved customers will have an impact. It is not good enough or fair for you to slag off a company in the abstract if you have not given to those concerned your views on the subject that is eating you.

The purpose of this book is to expand your mind (as they used to say in the 1960s). If you have never complained before, you will realise after your first success that the taste of victory is sweet and that it will affect you like a potent addictive drug. After your first result you will never suffer in silence again. When your postman arrives with a personal apology from the Managing Director and a fat compensatory cheque, you will not just feel better: you will feel liberated. It is not difficult to achieve that kind of success and when you do, you will change from a shy, twitching baby bunny into an assertive self-respecting adult. I hope that after reading this book you will feel confident and able to challenge the biggest and the best. Be it Tesco or Thomson, ICI or British Airways, you will have no excuse for inertia.

You can keep up to date with 'The Complainer' by reading his column every week in Saturday's Express *and by visiting his new website at www.complainer.co.uk.*

1
Leaving on a Jet Plane

(Air Travel)

Apart from getting divorced, having your right leg amputated and watching England lose to Germany at football, there are few things in life more stressful than travelling somewhere by aeroplane.

From a complaining point of view the best thing that can possibly happen to you is that your plane crashes with no survivors. When your 767 smashes into the side of a mountain it really is time to say enough is enough and assert your rights as a consumer. The problem is that at the very moment when life deals you an opportunity to whinge like never before and to get free first-class travel for life, you find that your typing fingers have become irretrievably detached from the rest of your body. Whereas a plunge into the Appalachians is likely to cause quite inordinate disruption to your journey, when it comes to air travel, other factors are constantly at work, creating setbacks of an equally irritating (albeit less fatal) nature.

What Goes Wrong with Air Travel?
❏ Delays are the most common source of grief. When you are strapped into your economy seat at Athens

airport, with nothing more than piped muzak and warm orange-juice concentrate to pacify you, the last thing you need is an unforeseen hold-up due to 'technical problems'. All too often, this is precisely what you will be given. I was once waiting for an aeroplane allegedly bound for Boston. The inevitable announcement was made via the public-address system that the flight had been delayed due to 'technical problems' with the cargo door. In order to speed up the departure process the passengers were invited on to the plane while Aer Lingus's highly trained engineers and technicians sorted out the gremlin. My seat was in a position that enabled me to see precisely what the engineers were doing. The harsh reality was that a couple of burly guys were busy whacking the cargo door with a sledgehammer. Now that's what I call technical.

❑ Another major problem is lost luggage. It comes as no shock to discover that after breakfast in London and lunch in Dubai your luggage has made it, with consummate ease, to Timbuktu. Of course you can (and probably should) buy insurance to cover this eventuality, but don't be drawn into thinking that insurance is some kind of panacea. It's not. For starters you will inevitably end up having a row with the miserly insurance company and, in any event, why should the airline lose your bag of designer underwear and then blame you for not insuring it?

Lost luggage illustrates perfectly the contempt with which far too many airlines regard their unsuspecting customers. The problem is frequently treated with stunning indifference. The passenger will fill out a form, hand it to a grumpy ground stewardess and then become sucked into 'the System'. The system is not human but computer-driven and if you're lucky it will process your grievance and spew out your suitcases three days later. If you're unlucky it will shrug its shoulders, mumble the word 'insurance' and politely inform you that under the Warsaw Convention (set out in minuscule print on the back of your ticket) your rights to compensation won't buy you the price of a packet of crisps.

❏ The other classic source of complaints about air travel is the food. Like cholera, Bernard Manning and traffic jams in the Watford one-way system, airline food should be avoided. On cockroach class it still involves rolls made from play dough and fake cream of the school-dinner-cum-shaving-foam variety. On Club Class (I've never known why it is called by this absurd name) the food is usually rich and processed and needs to be washed down with the freely available buckets of Californian Chardonnay. The medicinal value of the booze is so good that after a mere fifteen minutes you feel so wonderful that you want to join the Mile High Club forthwith. After forty-five minutes you are so dehydrated that your head starts to implode; you panic because you think that the aeroplane is banking steeply to the right (when it's not) and the once-friendly stewardesses (who plied you with alcohol in the first place) start marking your card as a troublemaker. As for First Class, the food is not rich but you have to be.

What Can You Do to Get Your Own Back?

What can you do to arm yourself against the rotten treatment dished out by even the most respectable of airlines?

❏ Be firm and polite but very assertive in situations of potential conflict. When the ground staff tell you to hand over your excessively bulky items of hand baggage for storage in the hold, tell them that it contains your most treasured jewellery and life-preserving heart tablets. Do not necessarily submit to the voice of authority. Lie if necessary.

❏ Take names. If a member of the aircrew is rude or unpleasant the last thing you should do is swing a punch or hurl abuse. Smile back at the gorgeous but obnoxious Barbie doll, ask for her name and save it for later. Information is the ammunition of a good complainer.

❏ When you write to Virgin Atlantic, for example, do not necessarily write to Richard Branson. He gets far too much post as it is and may ignore you. Write perhaps instead to his number two or three. They have very small in-trays and believe me, in this department, size matters. They just love the very idea of receiving the same kind of mail that is sent to their boss on a daily basis. They will rise to the occasion by responding promptly (a) to show Richard what goody-goodies they are and (b) because they are bored.

❏ If you don't like the disgusting airline food, send it to the Managing Director. My daughter had some rotten grapes on a British Airways flight back from Toronto. I sent the poisonous fruit to Bob Ayling, the (now ex) Managing Director of BA, with stunning effect. She and I were invited to don white coats and carry out an inspection of the catering facilities at Heathrow. We duly obliged.

❏ Whether it is brought about by the partially reheated Beef Surprise or by your friend and mine, 'turbulence', you may wish to comment openly about your state of nausea. Do not express yourself by throwing up over the cabin staff. They tend to react by either arresting you or by offering you a stomach-settling glass of liver salts. I tend to save up my bile for my follow-up poison-pen letter, although I once upset Alitalia by enclosing a sick bag (albeit empty). Sending full sick bags through the post is, incidentally, a criminal offence.

❏ When asking for compensation from airlines, think big. You do not need to be palmed off with a handful of air miles and a polite apology. It is no skin off the nose of a mega-international airline to give you and your partner a couple of Club Class tickets to a destination of your choice. If you do receive compensation of this kind, continue to think big. Fiji is nice.

❏ Foreign airlines, more than any others, hate to be sued in the small claims court. If this is your last resort (excuse the pun) give them a large dose of the very medicine they detest. To sue a company in the small claims court is very easy. Go to your local county court, ask for a form, fill it in and away you go! You can have great fun. I once sued Delta Airlines for my friend Jerry. Delta Airlines in Atlanta, Georgia had no idea where the Watford County Court was and ignored the court summons. Jerry obtained what is called a default judgement for £500 – i.e. a court order requiring Delta to cough up or else. Jerry rather fancied the idea of seizing a jumbo or sending the bailiffs to Gatwick to grab the stewardesses' hats. Unfortunately for Jerry, Delta paid up.

What Kind of Results Can You Expect?

COMPLAINT	POSSIBLE RESULT
Horrendous delays combined with indifferent staff and seriously shabby treatment	Financial compensation or even free flights
Lost luggage	Very little, due to the nasty small print on your ticket
Physical injury	Financial compensation
Poor-quality food	Exceptionally a small freebie but usually nothing

Sample Letters

A hint of humour and the careful avoidance of legalese are a winning combination. The involvement of a child makes this case even more persuasive.

Henny Essenberg Esq
KLM UK
Liberator Road
Norwich
Norfolk
NR6 6ER

Dear Henny

I am the *Express* newspaper's Official Complainer and I write on behalf of one of our youngest readers, Joseph Arnander, aged 9 months. Joseph's problem concerns flight UK2355 from Stansted to Edinburgh on 15 July this year (see booking confirmation attached).

Although both of Joseph's parents are litigation lawyers, Joseph has expressed the wish to me that this matter be resolved by alternative dispute resolution. The issue in essence is this. Flight UK2355 was originally due to take off at 10.30a.m. This fitted in nicely with Joseph's early morning itinerary: a long nap, a soggy rusk and a quick perusal of some learned texts on the law of contract. At the very last moment 10.30a.m. was

---

unilaterally brought forward by you to 08.15a.m. Joseph expressed his displeasure to his parents by threatening to either sue them for millions or to engage in a bout of rebellious projectile vomiting.

Joseph's parents were forced to spend the night at a grotty hotel at Stansted Airport (see invoice attached). Even then he (and they) had to awaken from their beauty sleep at the crack of dawn. Notwithstanding his limited grasp of basic legal concepts, in particular the provisions of the Warsaw Convention, Joseph is not prepared to tolerate the idea that the large print giveth and the small print taketh away. Please therefore do not refer him to your standard terms and conditions. He won't understand them.

If you have small children they will advise you that what Joseph and his family need is a meaningful gesture of goodwill. I have no doubt that you will restore the faith of Joseph and our readers in the quality of service offered by your company.

Yours sincerely

Jasper Griegson

Immediate financial compensation and a profuse apology followed from KLM.

Why not try a spot of verse to lighten up the MD's day?

Robert Ayling
Managing Director British Airways plc
Speedbird House
London Heathrow Airport
Hounslow TW6 2JA

Dear Bob

My postbag has thrown up a fax from Mr M.
Levitt, a copy of which is enclosed. Allow me to
comment as follows:

The Levitts like to fly BA,
They think that it's the only way,
For short-haul flights and long-haul too,
They say that nothing else will do.

Accordingly they chose BA,
When jetting off to San Jose,
On their return the tale they tell,
Was nothing less than the Flight From Hell.

The plane was cramped – they realised when,
They saw it was a DC-10,
The three-hour delay was not much fun,
Nor was the diversion to San Juan!

After 90 minutes of stewing there,
It was plain the plane was going nowhere,
At 6.30a.m. just for a lark,
The passengers were told to disembark.

During four hours waiting no one slept a wink,
There was no information, no food or drink,
The lounge was dirty and very hot,
Did BA care? BA did not.

On board again the passengers flocked,
To the toilets that were permanently blocked,
For the Levitts this was the final straw,
I hardly need to add much more.

The Levitts' treatment,
Was a dastardly crime,
And on that note,
I'll end this rhyme.

I look forward to hearing from you.

Yours sincerely

Jasper Griegson

The poem led to an offer of two free Club Class tickets to anywhere in the world.

Always write to Mr Big by name.

A. Urena de Guan Esq
Iberia International Airlines
27–29 Glasshouse Street
London W1R 6JU

Dear Mr Urena de Guan

I write on behalf of Simon Bennett of Hampshire.
 What do you not need from an airline when going for the holiday of a lifetime to Costa Rica? Let me tell you: a cancelled flight, an overbooked flight, an unwanted place in the smoking section, non-functioning headphones, a disinterested crew and a near miss! Is this the kind of fare normally dished up by Iberia to its customers or did the Bennetts merely encounter an extraordinary departure from your usual standards?
 We trust that your reply to this letter will not come in the form of a dismissive two-line apology from your Customer Services Department.

Yours sincerely

Jasper Griegson

Iberia responded with a full refund.

A pictorial approach sometimes helps to drive home the message.

Robert Ayling
British Airways plc
Waterside (HBB3)
PO Box 365
Harmondsworth
UB7 0GB

Dear Robert

As you may know, I am the *Express* newspaper's Official Complainer and I write on behalf of Sandra Trayte of London NW1. I have wondered for some time why your new budget subsidiary 'GO' was so named. I quite like its punchy brevity and I assumed that the name was designed to conjure up images of picking up one's bags and heading for the sun with consummate ease.

This is what Sandra and her husband thought as they arrived at Stansted Airport on 13th September. GO unfortunately took on a new significance for them when they were told to carry their suitcases to the aeroplane. The steward told them, just before boarding, to leave their suitcases behind on the runway. They duly obliged. Little did they think that the suitcases would then stay put for the next two weeks! Sandra and her husband most certainly did GO whereas their luggage, in stark contrast, did not.

Sandra's profound frustration has been captured in a picture drawn by my daughter Zoë, a copy of which is enclosed for you to hang on your wall. Incidentally, the stuff coming out of the nose is steam!

When replying, please ponder this question. Had the suitcases in question been yours, would the steward concerned have been hung, drawn and quartered by now? I look forward to hearing from you.

Yours sincerely

Jasper Griegson

British Airways paid £300 compensation to the Traytes.

2
We're All Going on a Summer Holiday

(Package Holidays)

Our leisure time is precious. We battle away all year against the onslaught of painful issues that life throws at us: unpleasant work colleagues, punctured tyres, the flu, overdrafts, the British climate and Geri Halliwell's ego. All have been very carefully designed by God to make us unhappy and depressed. But the human predicament is not a hopeless one. In the midst of the shadow of darkness there is a shaft of white light that shines out like a beacon of hope: holidays. Without a break from the toil of working life we would all go mad. Be it three weeks in Antigua or three days in Norfolk, we all need to have our batteries recharged now and again. Accordingly, when our cherished fortnight is ruined by a vile villa in Valencia or a horrible hotel in the Hebrides, we tend to get more upset about this than about anything else. Even the most placid non-complainer can become a rabid bull when locked into a disastrous holiday with no obvious escape route.

What Goes Wrong with Package Holidays?

Sod's Law dictates that the more desperately you need a holiday the more likely it is that your valuable vacation will be spoilt. What are the most common problems with package holidays?

❏ Holidays are widely oversold. The glossy brochures often raise the prospective holidaymaker's expectations to dizzy heights. This inevitably leads to upset and heartache. Whether it be the proximity of the beach (or rather the opposite), the shabby facilities or the quality of the accommodation, always be prepared for what I like to call the 'reality gap'. Expect the worst and you won't be disappointed.

❏ Non-existent or unhelpful reps are another common complaint. Reputable companies attempt, with the best will in the world, to hire enthusiastic reps. They often fail. A good ground force will sort out problems on the spot and keep the punters happy. But unfortunately, all too often the reps aren't fired up with the required keenness. Worse still, during their brief encounters with the holidaymakers they do little more than flog trips to places no one wants to visit.

❏ The food is frequently one of the sorest subjects. If you are staying at five-star accommodation you can be fairly sure, wherever you are, that the local fare will be tasty and well presented. As you slide down the scale of wonderfulness, expect the standards to plummet like a stone. When visiting anywhere other than the most civilised bits of western Europe I never stay on anything but a bed–and–breakfast basis. If you are locked into a fortnight's worth of gruel and pigswill, it does tend to spoil your sunny escape. You are far better off reserving your position by checking out the lie of the land and then exploring the local cuisine with your own eyes and nose.

❏ Dirt and decay are unacceptable, however cheap the holiday. Just because you bought your holiday at the last minute on the Internet for £250 doesn't entitle the holiday company to treat you like a dung beetle. I have heard stories of villas and hotel rooms that sound very much on a par with the kind of hospitality offered by debtors' prisons in Victorian times. Stinking sewers, showers blocked with human hair, stained bed sheets and flea–infested carpets are just a few of the delights unearthed by unsuspecting Britons abroad. Nothing of this nature is remotely tolerable. You have no desire to live in a zoo, so don't stand for anything that resembles one.

❏ Noise is another all–too–common complaint. A classic source of mega–decibel discomfort is the piledrivers operating ever so indiscreetly on the foundations of the half–built hotel next door. Another common complaint comes from sad Herberts like me who like to sleep at midnight rather than boogie at the all–night disco downstairs. In all seriousness, however, these are issues about which a warning should be given in advance. I have recently returned from a hotel in Eilat which was said to suffer from fallout from adjacent construction work. Having been warned, I braced myself for the worst but was pleasantly surprised – the disruption was minimal. Holiday companies should come clean but all too often don't.

What Can You Do to Get Your Own Back?

Holiday complaints are frequently very difficult to deal with. There is a huge temptation to lose your temper with the receptionist, the tour guide or the man who hands out the tickets for the pedalo. There is an equally great temptation to talk yourself into a state of total despair when things start to take a turn for the worse. However hot the climate or the dispute, it is imperative that you keep cool, even more so if your friends or family are losing theirs. You should rise above the problems and resolve to get your own back, even if you have already given up the ghost and gone home. If there is any way of salvaging even a modicum of pleasure from your holiday it is essential that you make this your first priority. Assuming you haven't given up and taken flight, don't descend into the depths of desperation by indulging in two weeks of self-pity and misery. If you can possibly do so, shrug your shoulders and laugh. Alternatively, shrug your shoulders and grin knowingly. If your room is inferior to the one shown in the brochure and the hotel refuses to upgrade you, remind yourself that you are there to enjoy your stay and that you will do that come what may. You will then relax, secure in the knowledge that you will receive compensation for your troubles on your return.

What else can you do, before and during the holiday, to make sure it's all you expect it to be?

❏ When you're on holiday you are unlikely to become the hostage of a hijacker. You are, however, quite often a hostage to fortune. When booking a package deal you invariably commit yourself to a raft of terms and conditions that you never read. Holiday companies will almost always reserve to themselves the unfettered discretion to change the arrangements – for example, forcing you to fly from Stansted Airport at 2a.m. rather than Gatwick Airport at 6a.m., or changing your hotel at your destination, often with little or no warning. Given that the fine print is non-negotiable, you are then stuck with the rearrangement and you should be acutely aware of this. By all means complain, but legally you don't have a suitcase to sit on. Don't go into a package holiday thinking you have not been pigeonholed. You have.

❏ Bearing in mind the 'reality gap', do your homework. Personal recommendations are 1000 per cent more reliable than the brochure photographs of azure blue seas and whitewashed villas. Photographers can do wonderful things with clever angles, tinted lenses and a hint of artistic licence. The twenty-four-hour drilling next door, the smell from the nearby sewage farm or the view of the adjacent graveyard never seem to come across properly in the glossy promotional literature. I wonder why not?

❏ Given that prevention is better than cure you may find that you are better off putting together a package yourself. Who needs holiday companies? Indeed, who needs travel agents? The Internet gives you the best possible tool for making your own arrangements. If you make a hotel booking yourself, you may well avoid having to make an upfront payment. This gives you some bargaining power if it all goes horribly wrong. One of the problems with package tours is that you have to pay in advance and often many months beforehand.

❏ When you're booking a holiday, never be conned into buying travel insurance from a travel agent. Shop around, find out what is covered by your credit-card scheme and discuss the details of whatever the travel agent is trying to shove down your throat. If he or she is too pushy or ignorant when asked about the details, give the agency's insurance a miss. There are a multitude of alternatives out there and you should never feel badgered.

❏ With holidays more than anything, you get what you pay for. If you book a cheapo package you can't expect the five-star touch. If, on the other hand, you have splashed out on the holiday of a lifetime with no expense spared, you have a right to expect more. If the plumbing in your cheap and cheerful hotel in Spain is noisy and unpredictable, it is unrealistic to expect massive compensation. If the plumbing in your room at the Plaza in New York is anything less than perfect, you should expect and demand the earth. It's horses for courses.

❏ If you have already booked your holiday through a travel company, be very careful to check the accuracy of what has been booked. Holiday companies make mistakes, computers make mistakes, airlines make mistakes – and prevention is better than cure. I have a recurring nightmare involving a last-minute attempt to board an aeroplane. It involves me sprinting down the main runway at Heathrow with bags and children in tow. Such drama is best avoided.

❏ When you're saddled with dirty or otherwise unsatisfactory accommodation or the hotel in general is below par, one good thing about being on holiday is that you are very likely to have a camera or video camera available to record the sordid details. I find that a spot of irrefutable empirical evidence goes a long way with big holiday companies. It isn't in their interests to have accommodation on their books that equals trouble just waiting to happen. When the Managing Director sees your revealing photographs or video of the overflowing drains or the rat-infested swimming pool he will welcome the information. Holiday companies pay lots of money to monitor the quality of their operation. A well-documented complaint will contain vital information, and such complaints are an excellent source of knowledge for them – and of redress for you.

❑ What should you do if, within five seconds of stepping into your room, you know that there is no way you can put up with the dungeon provided? If the powers that be refuse to move you, you have two options: (1) go home or (2) go to another hotel if you can. You shouldn't be afraid to cut your losses. You don't have to grin and bear it. You may still have an acceptable holiday and your claim for compensation will be based on the expense you were forced to incur.

❑ Reps are fair game as a first port of call when you have a complaint. In any case, when you are 3000 miles from home you are unlikely to be in a position to word-process and fax a complaint back to mission control. You have to have a go at attacking the problem on the spot. There are several reasons for this. First, the company will use it against you later if you didn't at least try 'the usual channels'. Secondly, even if the rep is useless, it is worth putting down a marker, as it makes it clear to the company (when you write on your return) that you aren't just angling for a post-holiday freebie. Finally, it might just work – some reps are hard-working and helpful.

❏ Holiday companies, more than any others, are geared to deal with complaints. They sell millions of package deals each year and they know that day in day out they are contending with emotions and pleasure and unsatisfied expectations. They therefore have teams of 'Customer Services Executives' dealing with the problem cases. At all costs you should aim to avoid the complaints sausage machine. This is geared to shutting you up with an offer of 10 per cent off your next booking. It is not designed to refund your money – at least not without a fight. If you can personalise your complaint in a way that circumvents the system, your efforts will reap handsome rewards. If you don't manage to do this, expect no more than a compensatory voucher and a profuse but platitudinous apology.

❏ In the event of a dispute, holiday companies encourage you to use the arbitration services operated by the industry regulators such as the Association of Independent Tour Operators (AITO) or the Association of British Travel Agents

(ABTA) (see page 254). I have found that these organisations are well-meaning but that their horizons are low in terms of compensation. For claims under £5000 the small claims court is a far better option: it is much more expensive for the holiday company; you have much more control over your destiny and the pace of the process; and, best of all, you face no costs if you lose. For claims over £5000, the ordinary county court system is worth considering if you are brave enough to risk having to pay the costs of the holiday company's legal bill should you lose the case. The simple truth is that holiday companies hate litigation and as a last resort you should hit them with a heavy dose of it if you really mean business.

❏ When formulating your letter of complaint, you should structure your demand under two distinct headings. The first should be for tangible losses – things with a price tag. This would include the cost of meals out if the food was disgusting or the cost of your dress if the hotel washing machine decides to shred it. The second is more vague – it is for inconvenience and lost enjoyment. The invisible reps, the vile decor, the noise from the all-night disco all fall into this category. If you ultimately end up in the small claims court it will be important to particularise your claim with as much detail and as many supporting receipts and other documents as you can.

❏ Don't be put off if the holiday company replies to your complaint by trying to shift the problem back on to you. The most common retort is that you should claim on your travel insurance for the lost luggage or the injury sustained in the hotel reception. Travel insurance is all very well but you buy it for your benefit, not in order to save the holiday company the cost of shelling out if it is at fault.

What Kind of Results Can You Expect?

COMPLAINT	POSSIBLE RESULT
A mixture of the usual package holiday complaints: rotten room, hopeless reps and bog-standard food	A few hundred pounds if there are extenuating circumstances relating to you rather than everyone
A major booking catastrophe resulting in a day's lost holiday	Again, a few hundred pounds at most
Accommodation that is so bad the holiday company agrees with you	Compensation approaching a full refund
Minor irritations such as the swimming pool being out of action for three days or the lifts not working properly	Vouchers for your next holiday or a very modest sum of money depending on your circumstances

Sample Letters

If a holiday is horrible enough, even a cheap one, it is possible to get all your money back or a free replacement holiday.

Stephen Haupt
Managing Director
Pontin's
Sagar House
Eccleston
Chorley
Lancashire PR7 5PH

Dear Stephen

I am the *Express* newspaper's Official Complainer and I write on behalf of Mr and Mrs McLoughlin of Wolverhampton.

What kind of imagery would you associate with a twentieth wedding anniversary? A sumptuous candlelit meal at a romantic Italian restaurant perhaps? A lavish bouquet of a dozen fragrant red roses? The clinking of glasses topped to the brim with vintage champagne?

The McLoughlins' anniversary celebration at Pontin's in Prestatyn was characterised by somewhat different features. The highlights were uncontrolled gangs of teenagers racing cars around the centre at 2.30a.m.; carving knives rammed into the grass outside the McLoughlins' chalet; under-aged drinking and drug-taking in the toilets and then, the crowning glory – pools of uncleared vomit just outside the reception area. These events, to say the least, dampened the fires of romance and sadly destroyed the McLoughlins' celebration of this special event. As you know, Mr McLoughlin has already raised other minor matters with you, including the lack of cleanliness.

Although your security staff were doubtless well-intentioned they were obviously ineffectual. I have no doubt that you will be as shocked as I was at what happened and that you will now take immediate action to address and redress the McLoughlins' shattered faith in Pontin's.

Yours sincerely

Jasper Griegson

Pontin's reply stressed that the company sees it as 'extremely important that our guests are satisfied with the outcome of any complaint' and in this spirit the McLoughlins were offered a free replacement holiday, which they accepted.

If it's really bad, there is no point in holding back on the detail.

A.H. Coe Esq
Managing Director
Airtours plc
Parkway One, Parkway Business Centre
300 Princess Road
Manchester M14 7QU

Dear Mr Coe

I am the *Express* newspaper's Official Complainer and I write on behalf of Hazel Doidge of Falkirk.

At her local travel agent, Hazel paid a substantial £1000 fine and was sentenced (together with her 10-year-old daughter) to two weeks of holiday (without remission). She thought that they would have a soft time and a quiet comfortable stretch in the sun. On their arrival at Le Panto Apartments in Spain the appointed jailer accompanied the prisoners to their designated wing, even demanding a £50 deposit for the jangling keys. Even by Iraqi standards the prison conditions would have shocked the most hardened criminal – small, shabby, squalid and stinking. The bars on the windows (I joke not) did obscure Hazel's view. She was, however, able to see, from the piles of broken bottles, cigarette ends and used condoms on the roof of the adjacent nightclub, that she was not the only person who had been banged up. Your rep was not around that day to offer a hint of parole and poor Hazel even had to suffer the stench of raw sewage around the drain in her bathroom.

After eventually finding and appealing to your rep, paying more money and lugging lots of luggage without help, Hazel and her daughter escaped to Escapades Apartments (again I joke not). It turned out to be a noisy detention centre and exercising in the yard was unpleasant because it was located in the middle of a building site and was surrounded by nasty bars of a different variety. After a fortnight of serving her time Hazel and her heartbroken little girl were released back into the community in England vowing never to reoffend with Airtours. ABTA aside, I feel Hazel ought to have a chat with the Howard League for Penal Reform. In the meantime I put it to you that these two victims should receive compensation for their disgraceful incarceration.

Yours sincerely

Jasper Griegson

PS: Does your brochure include the possibility of upgrading to mailbag sewing?

Hazel received a sizeable cheque.

If there are particular circumstances that you feel make your complaint all the more justified, you should emphasise this. A spoilt wedding anniversary is a good example.

John Donaldson
Chief Executive
Thomas Cook
45 Berkeley Street
London W1A 1EB

Dear John

I am the *Express* newspaper's Official Complainer and I write on behalf of Mr and Mrs Eccles of Middlesborough.

The Eccleses decided to celebrate their ruby wedding anniversary in style with a cruise on the TSS *Topaz* booked through your company. Mr Eccles ordered some flowers as a surprise arrival gift for his beloved wife and paid for them. They did not materialise.

Your reply to Mr Eccles's letter contained flowery language but was weedy in the extreme. It lacked anything resembling a heartfelt apology or a gesture of goodwill. Mr Eccles does not want to have his cake and eat it, he simply wants an apology and modest compensation. It would appear that the threshing machine that operates your complaints

---

procedure is chewing up correspondence, spitting out computer-generated replies and achieving nothing.

Mr Eccles is a romantic but not an incurable one. Please find an efficacious tonic to cure his malady without delay. Think big. Think romantic. Something studded with rubies and a chunky topaz would do nicely.

Yours sincerely

Jasper Griegson

The company apologised for the non-arrival of the flowers, admitting that 'There are no excuses for this', and for the subsequent delay in refunding the cost. By way of recompense a beautiful bouquet was rushed to Mrs Eccles at her home.

3
Lay Lady Lay

(Restaurants)

It is a curious feature of the human condition that we eat in restaurants at all. It is possible to feel entirely satiated at home on a bowl of Heinz tomato soup and a plate of egg and chips followed up by a king-size Mars Bar. If you aspire to a higher state of culinary consciousness you can buy a pretentious cookbook ghost-written by a famous chef and then, in the comfort of your own home, engage in a spot of DIY *haute cuisine*. As you serve your guests with stuffed mangetout nestling on a bed of honey-glazed seaweed you gain the added benefit of twenty-seven points for one-upmanship. Why, therefore, eat out in the first place? There is only one good reason. It is not the ambience. It is not 'the experience'. It is not even the company. It's the mess. Mankind knows of no challenge greater than that faced by the weary and inebriated hosts of a dinner party when the last guests have left at half past midnight. The stacks of pots, pans, glasses and plates is usually enough to make a grown man weep, even when aided by the most supersonically efficient German dishwasher. When you go to a restaurant you do not have to deal with the dishes unless your credit-card company catches up with you at a highly inopportune moment.

What Goes Wrong in Eateries?

Viewed objectively, eating out is a disaster waiting to happen, but what is the source of the diner's problems?

❏ Let's start with the food. I find it relatively hard to criticise the fare served up at fast-food chains. Why? Because my expectation level is so low that the restaurant will make it to first base if it manages to serve up a half-heated burger devoid of mouse droppings. In many ways I find the restaurants at the next level up far more irritating. It is not difficult to spend £45 per head at a lousy 'Italian' place in Fulham only to find that the uninterested staff have dished up watery minestrone, mushy microwaved vegetables and half-defrosted dessert. When the bill arrives at this kind of restaurant it inevitably includes a 12½ per cent service charge, a 5 per cent cover charge and a 5 per cent surcharge for 'extra ambience'. I could probably tolerate all of those things if it weren't for the waiters coming to my table every ten minutes with a large grin and a pepper-grinder the size of a baseball bat, offering to spice up my life.

❏ As one moves into the gastronomic stratosphere, expectations rise, along with the price. If I am stupid enough to spend £100 per head for the benefit of Marco Pierre White or Gordon Ramsay I am entitled to expect perfection. Anything less will not do. When I noticed that Marco's menus at the Criterion in Piccadilly had incorrectly described the coffee as 'expresso' rather than 'espresso', I complained, enclosing the relevant extract from *Collins Italian Dictionary*. Marco begrudgingly changed all the menus. I complained about this because (a) at that price nothing escapes my eye for detail and (b) the pleasure derived from winding up Mr Grumpy is in itself worth at least fifty quid.

❏ Ignore the apparent quality of the food for a moment and dwell, if you can bear it, on the dreaded subject that no one eating at a restaurant likes to think about for more than a nanosecond. Hygiene. Do cooks scrub their hands like surgeons? Do mice and cockroaches avoid the store rooms at expensively located three-star restaurants? Do aggrieved underpaid waiters resist the occasional temptation to spit in the food of a moaning guest? I don't think so. The only way to deal with these issues is to turn a blind eye, because the simple truth is that restaurant kitchens are disgusting. If you can smoke and think it's good for you or if you can munch an Aero bar and convince yourself that it forms part of your calorie-controlled diet because of the air bubbles, then you'll be fine. But if you are not well-practised in the art of self-delusion then you will not be able to consume your consommé without thinking of where the chef's fingers have been during the past twenty-four hours.

❏ And then there is the question of service. At Burger King I am happy if they manage to get the order right. At the Ritz I expect subservience of a kind unseen since the days of the Raj. If the food is wonderful but the waitress is elusive, slow and, when she does finally appear, surly, it can rather spoil what might otherwise have been a romantic soirée. It never fails to amaze me how a human being, whose tips are entirely dependent on the goodwill that he or she generates among the customers, can possibly afford to wear a funereal expression and filthy fingernails.

❏ The other issue that really gets my goat at eating establishments in this country is the mathematics. The bill is all too often completely incorrect and, for some reason, the numbers always seem to benefit the restaurant. Don't these people have calculators? The truth is that they do but that they cannot resist the temptation to rip off their unsuspecting patrons. There is, incidentally, a direct correlation between the size of the 'mistake' and the amount of alcohol consumed at the table. A party of twelve Yuletide boozers is no more capable of checking the bill than an eight-month-old child. And funnily enough, the restaurant owners know this.

What Can You Do to Get Your Own Back?

The waiters have the charm and smell of bad-tempered gorillas. The food isn't fit for a desensitised warthog. The 'atmosphere' can only be described as a smoke-filled stench. What can you do?

❏ The first rule is that you should attempt to enjoy yourself as much as possible on the spot, however bad it gets. If you spend the entirety of the meal fuming about the position of your table and bemoaning the disgusting state of the cutlery, there is no point in being there. The trick is to laugh at your dilemma and makes notes, mental or otherwise.

❏ If you can possibly avoid it, do not complain on the spot. You get better results this way. Allow me to explain. A few years ago my wife and I went with my mate Fatso and his wife to a celebratory meal at Raymond Blanc's eating house, Le Manoir aux Quat' Saisons. Fatso (who likes his grub) rather hoped that, because I was present, there would be something to complain about and the meal would be free. Not so. The starters were sumptuous, the main courses magnificent and the desserts divine. No cause for complaint. When we were finally served with coffee and petits fours, however, the Devil intervened. I crunched into a violet truffle only to discover human hairs running all the way through it. As I announced this discovery, Fatso's arms shot into the air and he whooped with the sort of delight normally reserved for the scorers of FA Cup-winning goals. Had I complained to the waiter, doubtless we would have been given a 10 per cent reduction from the bill. I opted to post the offending article to Raymond the following day. Horrified, he immediately invited us back for a wonderful replacement meal.

❑ If your restaurant meal consists of soup à la cockroach with week-old bread, and steak made of saddle leather, should you pay? If you pay nothing and try to leave the restaurant you will probably commit the criminal offence of 'making off without payment'. Unless you fancy a bit of do-it-yourself Rumpole and a night in a cell, this course of action is best avoided. If, on the other hand, you pay the restaurant a sum which you think represents the value of the meal and leave your name and address, the police (if called) will not intervene in what they will regard as a civil dispute. A pound will do the trick. In theory the restaurant could bring a civil claim against you for the balance but, given the amounts involved, it rarely will.

❑ Always 'go to the very top', however big the organisation. If you don't like your McNuggets, send them to the President of McDonald's in Illinois. This always guarantees an interesting result.

❑ You might imagine that because your ratatouille has been served with traces of rat that your first recourse should be to Trading Standards or your local health inspector. This may help others but it will not necessarily help you. Restaurants know that the statutory powers wielded by such bodies are draconian in the extreme and the unspoken threat is often the most potent weapon of all. Financial compensation and a profuse apology are usually enough to buy my silence unless I am so appalled that I feel that the public at large needs to know.

❏ Be wary of accepting a replacement meal as compensation. If you return to the restaurant with a beaming smile and dollar signs in your eyes, the chances of the staff spitting in your food increase by a factor of twenty. If you are prepared to risk it, free food does taste good and the taste is always enhanced by the sight of bow-backed waiters grovelling to sweep up your crumbs and top up your wine glass.

❏ Do not be afraid to complain about over-service. This is a concept barely recognised by the undiscerning customer but it can become every bit as annoying as poor service. The waiters at supposedly upmarket restaurants who swipe my plate away while I am still swallowing my last morsel of food always remind me of the Wimpy Bars of my youth. Over-chatty or over-friendly staff can destroy a meal. Your aim is to eat and enjoy the privacy of your chosen company – you do not want to hear about the waitress's boyfriend problems or the chef's incurable chronic dandruff.

❏ If you want to know whether or not to put your hygiene sensors on red alert, visit the toilet on your arrival. If the sinks and mirrors are cracked, grubby and caked with dirt–impregnated limescale you have a problem. The same low standards will almost certainly apply in the kitchen. If you're feeling really bold, ask to see the kitchen. A top–quality restaurant will proudly show off its commitment to cleanliness. On the whole, adopting the 'out of sight, out of mind' approach is probably the only way to enjoy yourself.

❏ Flattery will get you everywhere. If you have eaten at the restaurant before and you liked it, it is always worth saying so. If your letter employs phrases like 'an extraordinary departure from your usual high standards', this will usually work wonders.

What Kind of Results Can You Expect?

COMPLAINT	POSSIBLE RESULT
Food containing foreign objects (dead or alive)	Full refund plus a gesture of goodwill on top
Poor-quality food	Replacement meal or partial refund
Poor service	Replacement meal or partial refund
Delays	A compensatory cheque or credit voucher
Food poisoning	Very often, nothing – restaurants will rarely admit that it was their fault and proving it is very hard
The decor or setting is deeply unattractive	Nothing – don't bother. The restaurant owner likes flock wallpaper

Sample Letters

Flattery will get you everywhere.

Andrew Taylor
Managing Director
McDonald's Restaurants Ltd
Head Office
High Street
Finchley
London N2 8AW

Dear Andrew

Re: Fasting

I am the *Express* newspaper's Official Complainer
and I write on behalf of Debbie Schofield of
Newcastle-upon-Tyne.

Like me, Debbie is a bit of a McDonald's fan.
To be quite honest – a big Mac, large fries and a diet
coke will do me anytime. Who needs Le Manoir
aux Quat' Saisons or Le Gavroche when you can
have quarter pounders with cheese served by people
with smiles and shiny badges? This said, committed
though I am to the pursuit of McHappiness through
visiting your gastronomic temples, I do like my
burgers hot and quick. Don't you?

Debbie and her kids had to wait 40 minutes at
your Westerhope restaurant for what turned out to

be cold food. This was obviously a wild deviation from your usual high standards and for this reason I felt duty-bound to copy this letter to (a) Jim Cantalupo, the Chairman of the McDonald's Corporation in Illinois and (b) Ronald McDonald himself.

Please demonstrate to Debbie's family that in the context of service at McDonald's, 'fast' means swift. In Debbie's case 'fast' seemed to have acquired its hungrier meaning – at least whilst she and her family waited patiently, starving and salivating like Pavlovian dogs. I look forward to hearing from you.

Yours sincerely

Jasper McGriegson

Debbie and her family received a suitably penitent letter from McDonald's Senior Customer Services Manager, who had taken up the matter with the manager of the branch in question – plus £20 worth of complimentary vouchers.

Make the Chairman concentrate on your particular
problem above all else.

Julian Metcalfe
Chairman
Pret a Manger
16 Palace Street
Victoria
London SW1E 5PT

Dear Julian

I am the *Express* newspaper's Official Complainer
and I write on behalf of Mr J. Asquith of Watford,
Hertfordshire. Shut your eyes. Then think of the
following:
    Chips with mint ice cream.
    Steak and cranberry jam.
    Mushroom blancmange.
    Yucky, eh!
    Mr Asquith's devotion to your stores is almost
religious in its intensity. He worships your
chocolate croissants and regards your brie baguettes
as nothing short of divine. Best of all he adores
your Greek-style honey and muesli yoghurts, an
empty pot of which (purchased at your Ludgate
Circus branch) I enclose. When I say empty, in fact
I mean empty save for the piece of pasta also
enclosed which he found in it. How on earth did

Roman remains manage to invade Mr Asquith's Greek delicacy? History tells us that these two cultures are mutually incompatible.

Doubtless your technicians will reveal all. I assume that the offending item is not the remains of a maggot!

I look forward to hearing from you.

Yours sincerely

Jasper Griegson

Pret a Manger's Chairman replied to Mr Asquith, expressing his horror at this 'embarrassing situation', which, he said without further explanation, must have happened during the morning's production. He offered his profound apologies and vouchers 'to cover the money you wasted'.

Remind the company concerned about the obvious: loyal customers are ones to be kept happy.

David Thomas
Group Chief Executive
Whitbread plc
Chiswell Street
London EC1Y 4SD

Dear David

I write on behalf of Mr R.D. Prince of Hornchurch, Essex.

Every six weeks, for the past four years or so Mr Prince has treated his family to a Sunday lunch at his local Beefeater restaurant, The Dick Turpin.

Following their most recent meal (on 24th October) they felt as though they had been robbed in true Dick Turpin style. Why? Mr Prince's wife was happily enjoying a plate of potato skins when she realised that she was about to eat the skin of something less vegetable in nature than a spud. Lurking within her delicious starter was a plump white maggot called Mervyn. As was clear from Mervyn's obese body, he enjoyed potato skins every bit as much as Mrs Prince. Mrs Prince was less than enamoured at the prospect of sharing the dish with Mervyn and was even less keen on the concept of eating him. Mervyn concurred since being chewed like a piece of rubbery macaroni would almost certainly have ruined his career prospects: he was hoping to be elected to the post of Mayor and Chief Dung Monitor in Bluebottle City's forthcoming elections.

On the day, your restaurant manager buzzed about a bit and then, as an act of generosity, deducted the price of the starter. I'm surprised he didn't charge extra for the maggot!

Notwithstanding the fact that the Princes' lunch was completely ruined, your company offered paltry compensation. Mr Prince does not want a prince's ransom but a £20 voucher is not what I would regard as princely compensation in the circumstances. This is surely no way to treat extremely loyal customers, is it?

As for Mervyn, he has instructed me to demand from you a cow pat, some French beef and two Jeffrey Archer novels.

Yours sincerely

Jasper Griegson

Mr Thomas replied that a Brand Audit of the restaurant in question had been carried out earlier the same month and 'all hygiene procedures were found to be in place'. The company was therefore at a loss to understand

how a 'foreign body' arrived in Mrs Prince's Crispy Potato Shell starter. However, apologising for the 'distress this incident has caused her', the Group Chief Executive sent the Princes £20 of Whitbread Leisure Vouchers

A complaint involving thirty-two people is thirty-two times more powerful.

Andrew Taylor
Managing Director
McDonald's Restaurants Ltd
Head Office
High Street
Finchley
N2 8AW

Dear Andrew

As you know I am the *Express* newspaper's Official Complainer. I write on behalf of Kirstie, Jonathan, Jade (x2), Jemma, Jason, Katie (x3), Sam (x2), Leanne, Sean (x2), Philip, Stephanie, Peter, Daniel (x2), Hannah, Andrew, Marcus, Luke, Ben, Edward, Chris (x2), Jordan (x2), Jack, Jadine, Francesca and last, but certainly not least, their teacher Miss Quinn.

These people appear to be my apprentices. They are a motley crew and sail under the banner of Year 4 at Filton Hill County Primary School of South Gloucestershire. Their letter, signed by the whole class is enclosed for your urgent attention.

Week in week out these young pirates go for excursions to their local McDonald's restaurants where, for a variety of reasons, standards appear to be plumbing hitherto uncharted depths. The complaints from the good ship Filton range from wrong orders to uncooked food and from overcharging to toyless happy meals.

The crew's captain, Miss Quinn, has steered her ship-mates in my direction in the hope that McDonald's will demonstrate to these discontented children that McDonald's puts quality and customer care first.

We await your prompt reply.

Yours sincerely

Jasper Griegson

Senior Customer Services Manager Alexis Dolling backed up her profuse apology to Miss Quinn and her young charges with gifts in kind, a donation and a promise of a PR visit: 'I have enclosed a selection of Lion King Happy Meal toys for your

pupils, with our compliments. We are pleased to be able to support your work with literacy by donating the enclosed cheque to enable the purchase of some books for the class. In addition, and as agreed, I am currently arranging for a representative of McDonald's to visit your class during literacy hour to discuss how we respond to customer feedback, good and bad.'

4
Ticket to Ride

(Rail Travel)

I'll come to the particular bugbears of rail travel in a moment, but the first thing to realise is that what's wrong with British Rail is that it doesn't exist. It was abolished and then sold off. Or was it sold off and then abolished? I can't remember. In any event its non-existence can be a problem, especially if you're hoping to catch the 07.55 to Hull.

In fact, whether British Rail ever existed is a moot point. Twenty-five years ago there was precious little evidence of a train service in this country. The occasional bone-rattler meandered out of Waterloo at its leisure but if you set your sights on a particular train it immediately became a ghost train. British Rail could cancel trains and then make them disappear with consummate ease. The situation is no better today. You might expect the 16.40 to Basingstoke to leave in five minutes time but it won't. Not if you really need to be in Basingstoke. It will be cancelled due to 'points failure' or 'signalling problems' or, most intriguing of all, 'an incident'. 'An incident' is the phrase used when a commuter has abandoned all hope of getting to Basingstoke on time and has decided to take the scenic route via heaven. 'Points failure' is the catch-all excuse employed when the railway operator can't think of anything more interesting to say.

Before British Rail was privatised we all knew where we stood. The reliability of the trains was appalling, the behaviour of the staff towards the passengers was horrible and the food served up at the buffet car was only fit for pigs, and pretty unfussy pigs at that. British Rail was predictably bad but it was at least a dowdy, dreadful devil that you knew. It was so deliciously awful that at times its awfulness was almost charming. The ticket collectors with their ill-fitting caps, the cheddar sandwiches with their curled edges and the Victorian rolling stock all combined to create British culture at its very worst. We were proud of it. And then suddenly all that was supposed to change. With the arrival of Mrs Thatcher, public ownership became a thought crime. The Great White Hope was that private companies would dust off the cobwebs and put the railways back on track, as it were.

Sadly, rail travel in the post-BR world is worse than ever. The reason is twofold. First, we believe falsely that someone like Richard Branson can run a railway with the same efficiency he runs other enterprises. He can't. Virgin trains seem to fail just like any other British trains. Secondly, our hopes were raised and then dashed. We used to know that trains were a waste of space and so kept our expectations low. Now we are encouraged to foster the quaint but baseless hope that things will improve. My advice is that you should still regard Britain's railway system as a shambolic, investment-starved farce. If you do, you will not be disappointed.

What Is Wrong with the Railway System?

❏ First, the trains don't run on time. This problem could easily be solved. If Great Western or Connex South Eastern were to employ a small, dark Austrian with a moustache, some radical expansion plans and a team of persuasive inspectors in leather trench coats, the trains would run on time. The root of the problem is that the English are not German or Swiss. We may drink Bavarian lager by the gallon and devour M&S Swiss chocolate by the lorryload, but the red stuff that fuels the Teutonic psyche does not course its way through our veins. Punctuality is not a British trait.

❏ The second problem is that even if the trains do run on time it is impossible to tell. The booklets containing timetable information do not make for light reading. *Gormenghast* in Dutch is easier to comprehend than Silverlink's Watford to Euston departure schedule. Moreover, the train that arrives at the time you expect may not in fact be going to a destination you expect, because often it is the wrong train. In addition, there are never any station announcements to alert you and there are no guards on the train to blow the whistle when you get your leg trapped in the door after realising at the last minute that you want to go to Crewe instead of Birmingham.

❏ The third problem is that the typical train is not a comfortable place to be. The train lavatories are invariably stuffed with enough toilet paper to sink a battleship, the flush never works and the door lock is always out of order. The seats are cramped and dirty and there is an unshakeable law which dictates that the more you want peace and quiet, the more likely it is that you will find yourself seated next to a garrulous twenty-three-stone Jehovah's Witness with a body-odour problem. The gangways are filled with people queuing for the sparsely stocked buffet car, tired travellers without seats and other assorted busybodies.

❏ The fourth most common problem is the refreshments. I use the word cautiously. Like the train itself, these will very often not exist. A train packed with parched passengers will happily leave Plymouth bound for London devoid of cold drinks. Usually, the excuse given for this extraordinary state of affairs is that it is due to factors 'beyond our control' or 'staff shortages' or even 'an incident'. As for the buffet food, this has pretensions of being something better than it is. The cheddar in the sandwiches will be described as 'farmhouse cheddar' but the 'farmhouse' bit will be incapable of detection by the human tongue. The contents of the 'oriental' chicken roll will originate from no further east than Gravesend and the 'freshly brewed' coffee will most certainly have been freshly brewed ... last Wednesday.

What Can You Do To Get Your Own Back?

Railway companies are notoriously difficult to deal with when it comes to complaining. They are in the business of getting bodies in bulk from Bolton to Bradford. They are not good at catering for individual needs, unless you travel (and pay for!) first class. Nevertheless, here are some useful tips:

❏ Do not be deflected by so-called Customer Charter refund schemes. The train companies' aim is to funnel the misery of their long-suffering passengers into pint-size containers that can then be quietly and fragrantly discarded out of harm's way. When something goes wrong, the companies would like you to fill out a form. They will then require you to sell your soul to the devil for the price of a measly ticket voucher. The form system does not operate for the benefit of the passengers but for the convenience of the 'Customer Services Executives' to whom all complaints are delegated.

❏ If the problem is personal, make it personal. You will often find that the root of your complaint is a rude or indifferent member of staff whose mind is much more focused on going home than getting you home. Name the employee and shame him. Train companies respond badly to very general complaints (most of which will involve the desirability of their investing £1 billion in new hardware).

❑ If the problem is slightly less macrocosmic than that of the replacement of 90 per cent of the company's rolling stock, you are in with a chance of success. A broad-brush complaint based on the fact that the company's trains are frequently delayed is unlikely to produce a result. A complaint that the door did not open and that you were imprisoned on the express to Edinburgh may meet with sympathy. It is a good idea to concentrate on the 'exceptional' nature of the problem. A bit of flattery with reference to this trauma 'being an extraordinary departure from your usual high standards' is always a good ploy.

❑ It is never a bad idea to ask for a copy of the company's general conditions of travel. This is the book referred to by that note on your ticket: 'see general conditions of travel for further details'. When you step on to a train you sign up to a series of infinitely boring terms. Clause 333(iii) (a) prevents you consuming a cucumber sandwich in the toilet on a Tuesday after 18.00 and clause 44(iv) (c) requires all blind passengers to brush their guide dog not less than two hours before departure. In the bad old days of British Rail the book of general conditions rivalled *Crime and Punishment* for length, last week's *Yorkshire Post* for usefulness and paint drying for excitement. Why ask for the tome from hell? Well, it costs the rail company from hell money to make the things, they provide excellent ammunition for really long and boring letters and they make excellent draught excluders.

❏ If all else fails, there is no harm in threatening direct action. I wanted a bench put in place on the southbound platform at my local tube station. London Underground wouldn't comply with my demand. I threatened to take a bench from my garden and put it in position if they did not submit. That threat, coupled with a drawing of me looking angry (produced by my youngest daughter), finally did the trick.

What Kind of Results Can You Expect?

COMPLAINT	POSSIBLE RESULT
Horrendous delays leading to dire personal consequences	Modest compensation. Free tickets if you're lucky and the delay was very serious
Disgusting conditions such as no heating or no refreshments	A travel voucher and, if you're really fortunate, a free ticket
Personal injury	Financial compensation after a war of attrition with the train company's insurers
Mishaps such as stuck doors or cock-ups over tickets	Travel vouchers and occasionally money

Sample Letters

A spot of colourful description is an excellent way to liven up a dull complaint.

Martin Ballinger
Go Ahead Group
Cale Cross House
Pilgrims Street
Newcastle upon Tyne
NE1 6SW

Dear Martin

I am the *Express* newspaper's Official Complainer and I write on behalf of Mr Murray Grainger of London N16.

The 4th September was a frosty autumnal morning and the high-powered young City solicitor, Mr Grainger, ambled through the ticket barrier at King's Cross Station. Little did the unsuspecting lawyer realise that he was about to become the 886th victim of a mechanical molesting monster. As he strode through the barrier the hideous sinewy arm of The Gate from Hell (more widely known as 'The Ripper') plunged its thrusting tentacles into Mr Grainger's right jacket pocket, shredding it. Whether the Ripper's true target was Mr Grainger's crown jewels will never be known – fortunately they were spared. The gaping hole left in Mr Grainger's garment and bank account (see the attached) has left him scarred for life. He has been diagnosed as suffering from a rare and debilitating medical condition known as TBS (ticket barrier syndrome). He quivers every time he even thinks of a ticket barrier. TBS can only be cured by the administration of copious compensation (see the attached again), combined with very large chocolate bars. Please arrange for industrial quantities of both to be sent to Mr Grainger forthwith.

Yours sincerely

Jasper Griegson

Thameslink, the body responsible for the ticket barriers at King's Cross, saw the funny side of the situation but stressed that this did not 'dispel the concern we have over what appears to have happened'. The company's Marketing and Communications Manager, Martin Walter, asked for Mr Grainger's help in identifying the errant machine. Compensation and chocolate, he assured the victim, would then be supplied 'to relieve your TBS'.

Conjure up the suffering with graphic explanation.

Ann Gloag
Executive Director
Stagecoach Holdings plc
Charlotte House
Charlotte Street
Perth PH1 5LL

Dear Ann

Re: South West Trains

I don't know about you but I think that there are few pleasures in life more enjoyable than a really hot sauna. As the perspiration builds up one feels the trials and tribulations of modern life melt away in a process of unashamedly epicurean catharsis. The best part is the cold shower afterwards followed by a relaxing slumber and a long iced ginger ale.

Some saunas are however less pleasant than this.

I write on behalf of Ms Angela D'Arcy of Marlborough, Wiltshire. Angela seems to be subjected to an unsolicited sauna every time she boards the South West commuter train from Waterloo to Andover. This happens because, more often than not, the air conditioning breaks down. Angela is heavily pregnant and finds the unwanted tropical climate extremely distressing. The occurrences have been all too frequent over the past fortnight.

Without wishing to get hot under the collar, Angela is steaming at the prospect of more balmy journeys when she pays more than £3000 per annum for her ticket. I think you owe it to all of your customers, particularly those carrying either babies or disabilities, to sort this out. Don't you?

Yours sincerely

Jasper Griegson

Graham Eccles, South West Trains' Managing Director, admitted that Ms D'Arcy had 'the misfortune to travel' on one of the Class 159 Diesel Multiple Units leased to the company by Porterbrook, also a subsidiary of the Stagecoach Group. The air conditioning in these carriages, he explained, had never worked properly and the solution was its wholesale replacement with a more efficient system. South West Trains had started to do this on a trial basis, but Mr Eccles would say no more than that, should the renewal prove viable, the cost of around £1 million would be 'money well spent'. It looks like no imminent improvements in comfort for travellers on the Andover–London line.

Dare to be different. Just because no one in the crowd has ever bothered to moan to the powers that be, there is nothing to stop you.

Peter Ford
Chairman
London Regional Transport
55 Broadway
London SW1H 0BD

Dear Peter

<u>Met Line Madness</u>

I am the *Express* newspaper's Official Complainer and I write on behalf of Mr Simon Black of Watford, Herts.

Mr Black does not wish to paint an unduly dark picture of your attempts to knock the Met line into shape. Indeed, he is the kind of man who will dance a lap of honour around the ticket machine at his local station when a new improvement is finally put into place. His joy reached a peak of euphoria when last year you finally installed some marvellously informative train indicators at Finchley Road Station. The orange radiance of the indicators' display lights was outshone only by Mr Black's glow of satisfaction at being able to tell when the semi-fast train to Watford is due to arrive.

So far so good. But no good if you stand on platform 1 at the front end. Why? Try it and see! The old non-functioning sign blocks the view of the new, brightly-lit technological wonder. No one at that end of the platform can see it. The old sign appears to be suspended in place by two thin pieces of metal. Would you mind if Mr Black and I nip down to the station with a ladder and a chain-saw to sort the wretched thing out at no charge? I've changed fluorescent light bulbs before.

I look forward to hearing from you.

Yours sincerely

Jasper Griegson

LRT declined my offer, but Mr Black's plea was heeded the following week, when the visual obstruction was removed.

Remind the company about any promises made in their own promotional literature.

Christopher Garnett
Chief Executive
Great North Eastern Railways
Station Road
York Y01 6HT

Dear Christopher

I am the *Express* newspaper's Official Complainer and I write on behalf of Mrs K. Hogg of West Linton, Peeblesshire.

Mrs Hogg's story is quite remarkable and I would be grateful if you personally would intervene to demonstrate that GNER is not managed by an uncaring, heartless bunch of jobsworth bureaucrats. I'm sure it isn't.

Mrs Hogg and her daughter boarded a train at Edinburgh bound for York. For starters there was a 90 minute delay but that was just the beginning of the most miserable and pointless trip of their lives. As the train pulled into York station the button to open the door would not work. They waved and screamed at a guard who responded by waving back! The next thing they knew, they were imprisoned on a non-stop trip to Peterborough. They made it to York five hours later. What was supposed to have been a relaxing day out turned into a frustrating nightmare.

Your response to date has been to bung Mrs Hogg a pathetic and derisory £10 travel voucher. Your website advert says that you listen to your customers' concerns. Please do so on this occasion with a massive gesture of goodwill.

Yours sincerely

Jasper Griegson

Mrs Hogg and her daughter were given two complimentary first-class return tickets to York to compensate them for what GNER admitted was a 'bad experience'.

Just because a complaint is funny doesn't mean it isn't serious.

Bill Dix
Managing Director
Eurotunnel Shuttle Services
St Martin's Plain
Cheriton
Folkestone
Kent CT19 4QD

Dear Bill

<u>Looless in a Shuttle</u>

I write on behalf of Barbara Michaels and her friend Valerie. I enclose their travel vouchers.

When trying to board the Eurostar on their return journey from Paris, Barbara and Valerie were held up by delays lasting an hour or so. The weather was awful and, although they needed to take a natural break, they decided to hold out until boarding in order to dodge the rain.

After such a long wait they were soon desperate to avail themselves of the nearest loo. Barbara headed for the toilet nearest to compartment 21. After waiting for what seemed like eternity with a crowd of others, a member of staff finally turned up and informed poor Barbara

---

71

that that loo was locked and broken. She was advised to scurry off to the upper deck. She obeyed only to discover that that loo was broken too.

I note that the recent banner headline of *Eurotunnel News* reads: 'Let Yourself Go'. At least Barbara and Valerie didn't do that.

Although Barbara eventually found solace in a loo in compartment 25, Valerie was still bursting and was forced to wait until exiting at Folkestone! She simply didn't share Barbara's stamina for what might be termed a wild loos chase.

Do me a favour, Bill. Neither Barbara nor Valerie is a spring chicken and a tiring excursion around the corridors of your train in search of a mythical WC was not their idea of fun. Please convince them that this is not normal.

My fingers are now emulating Barbara and Valerie's legs. They are crossed. I have done this in the hope that you will reply to this letter with humour and a gesture of goodwill.

Yours sincerely

Jasper Griegson

Along with the company's profound apologies, and an assurance that the no-loo problem was being addressed, Barbara and Valerie received vouchers for a free trip on Eurotunnel.

5
Money, Money, Money

(Banks)

Banks are horrible institutions because they are jam-packed with money and you can't have it. Worse than that, banks seem to have an insatiable appetite for more money (most notably yours) and instead of giving the stuff away (their swollen coffers could easily cope) they take it from you and don't give it back. Worse still, when they take it from you, they charge you for the pleasure.

What Is Wrong with the Banks?

The problems Joe Public encounters with banks are too numerous to list in a book as thin as this but here are some of their worse failings:

❏ Although many of the staff are courteous, helpful and sensible, you will occasionally come across a gormless idiot. The bean-counter from the planet Density is only alive in the same way that dandelions are alive. If you ask this person a textbook question like 'How long will it take for this cheque to clear?' you will receive a textbook answer, straight from page seventy-three of the bank's manual. If you ask a difficult question like 'Are you able to answer difficult questions?' you will encounter a blank expression. The silicon chip secretly planted inside the body of the teller during his 'induction course' at Head Office will start sending odd messages to his brain and lips: 'You have performed an illegal operation, please switch off and reboot immediately' or, alternatively: 'Can I interest you in our new high-interest-bearing Gold Account – it really is a little marvel.' Third World debt and punitive interest charges are among those areas which banks' counter staff find most troublesome. The simple truth is that they know less about banking than you or I do. Most of them have come straight out of college and are more interested in the price of spot-remover than the fact that £10,000 has been incorrectly debited from your current account.

❏ The next problem, which very much flows from the first, is that banks make mistakes by the shed load. If you are lucky enough to speak to a human (rather than a voice-activated computer) to protest about the error in question, the human will all too frequently blame the computer. This excuse is not acceptable! The bank is responsible for its own computers and can't pass the buck off into the void of cyberspace. When it makes a mistake, the bank will always seek to apportion blame away from itself. Many years ago Barclays Bank sent me an extremely stroppy letter in which they notified me that, in true Monopoly style, there was a bank error in my favour.

In error (theirs, but they did not admit it), £100 had been transferred into my account at NatWest. They demanded the return of the money. I decided to do unto Barclays as Barclays would do unto its customers. I sent them £90, deducting £10 for my administrative charges.

❏ This brings me to another serious complaint. Banks are worse than garages when it comes to hidden charges. If they send you a letter about your overdrawn account, they charge you £20 and make you even more overdrawn. If someone bounces a cheque on you, they charge you £25, presumably for allowing it to happen. If the bank manager sneezes, you can be charged £20 for coughing imprudently at your local branch. When you complain about these charges, you will be shown the beautifully printed, crystal-clear small print on the basis of which you opened your account four years earlier. Clause 17(d) (iv), for example, entitles the bank 'in the event of any default' to take your wife as collateral and sell her off into slavery for a pittance.

❏ The big issue with banks at the moment is that they are becoming more and more virtual – i.e. less and less actual. Long gone are the days when you could butter up your bank manager with a good stoke-up and a few stiff gins. The main problem arising from this situation is that your bank manager has, by now, almost certainly ceased to exist. Centralisation, computerisation and modernisation have produced Frankenstein's baby: an abomination. Humans have been replaced by computers, letters have been replaced by forms and the art of conversation has been replaced by push-button options on your telephone. If you want to obtain your current account balance, press 1. If you want to order a cheque book, press 2. If you want to speak to the manager you can press any number you choose. It won't help because he has been vaporised. Banks have been administratively cleansed so that there is very little human activity separating the ciphers at branch level from the bigwigs at head office. *Homo sapiens* has gone. Only aliens remain.

❑ The worst thing of all about banks is that they lend you money and then get extremely unhappy when you can't repay it as quickly they would like. It's all smiles and handshakes when they hand over the dosh. When it comes to rescheduling your long-term debt two years down the line, the lending manager metamorphoses into a cross between a headmaster and Count Dracula. When you tell him where he can shove his loan, matters rarely improve. His vampire features come to the fore and the bloodsucking begins.

What Can You Do to Get Your Own Back?

If you were unlucky enough to encounter a lobotomised sheep at branch level who has screwed up your account for the umpteenth time, or if the bank decides to repossess your house even though you have never been overdrawn in your life, what can you do?

❏ If you owe the bank money, make sure you owe it lots of money. It will then treat you with respect. If you are a South American dictatorship, hopelessly in arrears and billions in debt, you do not have a problem. You will be invited to discuss matters over lunch in the restaurants of London's top hotels and top bank officials will fall over themselves to be nice to you. If you are a student whose grant cheque has arrived late and who needs £50 to buy some basic groceries, you will be grilled by an officious 'student loans liaison officer' and will receive nasty letters as soon as you overstep the mark by £10.

❏ If you owe the bank money but the amounts involved are in dispute, your best course of action is to write very long and tedious letters that demand equally long and tedious replies. Banks hate letters. Letters require human thought, which, for the reasons described above, they are incapable of generating. It will take the bank three weeks to find someone who is brave enough to write a human response, a further two weeks for that person to compose his or her masterpiece and a further three weeks after that for a secretary to be found. The Chairman of Lloyds TSB has a long-serving, highly devoted and efficient secretary. Everyone else in the organisation has to scramble around for a temp.

❏ Be realistic about what the bank will give you as compensation. It is no skin off the nose of a fast-food chain to give you a free burger. It is not hard for Marks & Spencer to replace your defective blue shirt. The only thing that banks have to give away is money and they hate doing that. It's against their religion. They are not averse to writing off debt now and again but they are very unlikely to hand over filthy lucre as a gesture of goodwill. For starters they don't care enough, but in any event it goes against the grain. I have, in the past, asked the chairman and chief executive of a large and prestigious bank for a wheelbarrow full of chocolate buttons. I have yet to receive anything of that kind. I live in the hope that Cadbury's will one day move into financial services.

❏ Do not be afraid to impose your own terms. You may not always get away with claiming for your own administrative charges but you need not be pushed around. Tell the bank that the mortgage you want is the one offered by their closest and most bitter rival. It's amazing how flexible a bank can be when you threaten to close down your accounts, change your pensions and switch your mortgage. For those who moan loud enough to the people at the top, there are individuals working to keep the customers happy.

This is not motivated by the milk of human kindness but by a solitary word written in tablets of stone in language that every banker understands: profit. If you touch a raw nerve, banks can be very sensitive to competition and they need to be reminded about this. The obvious truth is that there is very little to choose between the main high-street banks. Like petrol stations, they are much of a muchness in terms of products, efficiency and price.

❏ Never labour under the misconception that you have a 'relationship' with your bank and that you should not upset your bank for fear of upsetting that 'relationship'. There was a time when a bank would assess your standing in the community, your personality and your integrity on a one-to-one level. The harsh reality now is that, whatever you request, your plea is assessed on a points system by a throbbing great computer that wouldn't know the difference between you and a cardboard box if it weren't for the data shoved into it. Accordingly, you should feel free to complain with impunity and to 'bed-hop' when the need arises. There is always another bank or credit-card company desperate for your custom.

❏ Banks aside, the whole world of personal finance, investments, insurance, mortgages and pensions is a minefield. Without professional advice or at least some guidance from a watchdog or professional body (see page 251) the layperson may encounter insuperable obstacles. Whatever you do, don't ignore the problem.

What Kind of Results Can You Expect?

COMPLAINT	POSSIBLE RESULT
Overcharges	These will be refunded with interest and a curt apology
Poor investment advice	Banks will rarely admit liability of this kind without the threat of legal action
Poor service	Nothing. Banks hate to write out cheques in favour of their customers. Banks are generally payees rather than payers
Rudeness and indifference	Nothing. For far too long the banks have prided themselves on a contempt for their customers
Bank errors in your favour	Banks will not push for interest or for immediate repayment, but if you don't repay they will happily sue you

Sample Letters

Banks hate giving money back. If they rob you, remind them whose money it is.

G.R. Mathewson Esq
Chief Executive
Royal Bank of Scotland

Dear Mr Mathewson

Internet Raid

As you know, I am the *Express* newspaper's Official Complainer and I write on behalf of Mr Perry of Rickmansworth, Herts.

Mr Perry holds an RBS Advanta credit card which for the last two years has been fleeced to the tune of £12.23 per month by a mysterious monthly payment. The sums in question appear to go to an Internet company in America called IBL. Given that Mr Perry (a) is totally unnerdy (b) does not own an anorak and (c) does not possess a computer connected to the Internet, it is plain that he is being robbed. He is currently down by approximately £250.00 and I would be grateful if you would ensure that he gets it back. That kind of money buys 700–odd Mars bars, 200 jars of Nutella or approximately 650 Crunchies. It's serious!

In order to expedite matters you may wish to give Bill Gates a quick buzz. You can try calling him on 001-425-882-8080.

I await your prompt response.

Yours sincerely

Jasper Griegson

The Royal Bank of Scotland repaid the full amount to Mr Perry.

Remind your bank that it is not a monopoly. You can always take your account elsewhere.

Christopher Rodrigues
Group Chief Executive
Bradford & Bingley Building Society
PO Box 88
Croft Road
Crossflatts
Bingley BD16 2UA

Dear Christopher

I am the *Express* newspaper's Official Complainer and I write on behalf of Liz McHardy of Dinaspowys.

What is your favourite board game? On a rainy afternoon I am rather partial to a protracted and bitterly contested game of Monopoly. Few things are more satisfying in life than building a hotel on Mayfair and then having your worst enemy land on it. Do you recall that Community Chest card that gives you £200 due to 'a bank error in your favour'? So much for games. Liz seems to have been dealt a similar card by the Bradford & Bingley Building Society. The problem is that it reads as follows:

Building Society Error Not in Your Favour – Lose £500.

After generating enough correspondence to clear a Canadian forest and after spending a prince's ransom on telephone calls, Liz is no further forward to recovering her missing £500. You have given her a runaround of marathon proportions and she has, to put it bluntly, had it up to her eyeballs with the Bradford & Bingley.

Please ensure that the pen-pushing bureaucrats within your organisation are given a good caning. Thereafter they should be directed to sort this problem out with lightning speed.

I look forward to hearing from you.

Yours sincerely

Jasper Griegson

Mrs McHardy's £500 was traced and returned to her account, along with interest backdated over the two years since she had opened it. To the best of the Society's knowledge, a letter from the Group Press Officer explained, a computer error of this kind had never occurred at the Bradford & Bingley before.

If your banking problem doesn't involve the bank coughing up any money it will normally respond well.

Sir Peter Middleton
Chairman Barclays Bank plc
54 Lombard Street
London EC3P 3AH

Dear Sir Peter

I write on behalf of Miss J.S. Butler of Longfield, Kent, whose poem to me is enclosed.

Poor Miss Butler says it all,
She's being forced to lose her cool,
The junk mail which she gets each day,
It seems will never go away.
That Barclaycard is so intent,
On posting stuff that shouldn't be sent,
Is irritating and most unfunny,
And furthermore a waste of money.
Please tell Miss Butler you've made sure,
That no more junk will darken her door.

Yours sincerely

Jasper Griegson

Barclays apologised and explained that Ms Butler's address had now been added to their 'suppression list', ensuring that no future mailings to her would be generated.

Insurance companies are the same as banks. They love taking money from you and they hate giving it back. It is possible to make headway on your own but if you can't obtain satisfaction you may need to seek help from a third party or a lawyer. Alternatively, the Insurance Ombudsman (see page 263) may be able to assist you.

Raymond Treen
Chief Executive
Cornhill Insurance plc
Cornhill House
6 Vale Avenue
Tunbridge Wells
Kent TN1 1EH

Dear Raymond

A Mouse in the House

I write on behalf of Mr A. J. Lang of Southfields, London.

Mr Lang took out an insurance policy to cover

the possibility of his dishwasher breaking down. Your company has refused to cough up for some damage caused to the said appliance by Mervyn.

Who, you might ask, is Mervyn?

Mervyn is the delinquent half-brother of Mickey Mouse, a creature so hell-bent on destruction that he is widely regarded in the underworld as the rodent equivalent of Ronnie Kray. Mervyn wrought havoc on Mr Lang's sump hose so as to wreck the machine and cause a dirty-dish pile-up of Everest proportions.

Instead of reaching for their cheque-book, your legalistic claims boys have sought refuge in the haven of an exclusion clause. Mervyn, they say, is a 'foreign object' for the purposes of clause 2(e). I have discussed this with Mervyn and I can assure you that, unlike his Yankee relation, he is English through and through. He is no more foreign than Cheddar Cheese, Big Ben or the Union Jack.

Please tell those concerned that for the purposes of clause 1 of the policy, Mr Lang's dishwasher did most certainly suffer a breakdown. Please pay up before Mr Lang does likewise.

Yours sincerely

Jasper Griegson

Cornhill paid Mr Lang's claim in full.

6
Could It Be Forever?

(Consumer Durables)

In biblical times people worshipped God. The heathens who didn't worship God worshipped golden calves. God meted out appropriate punishment to the heathens, like turning them into pillars of salt or making them into Arsenal supporters. That was usually the end of the matter. In modern Britain people stopped worshipping God because churches have been replaced by DIY stores and garden centres. Unguided by a spiritual divine force, the British have turned their attention in another direction. Given the paucity of golden calves in the Argos catalogue, they have opted for the next best thing: white elephants. The British mission in life is to go to an out-of-town shopping centre and buy so-called white goods: be it a fridge, a cooker, a dishwasher or a tumble-dryer, the British appetite for dull household obelisks is insatiable. Less white things, like vacuum cleaners and food-processors, are added to the hit list if the consumer in question is genuinely well stocked with lots of white things. Like the proverbial painting of the Forth Bridge, the mission to keep up with the consumer durables marketplace (let alone the Joneses) is a never-ending one.

What Goes Wrong with Consumer Durables?

❏ The companies that sell white elephants make sure that as soon as you have bought the very latest design in frost-free fridge-freezers, a newer and better version will appear on the market. It will be bigger and better in every way and will include an ice-dispenser to die for. You are thus forced into a state of non-stop salivation.

❏ The companies that sell white elephants make very sure that the creatures to whom they give birth have hidden, undetectable genetic disorders that kill the elephant within five years. In the olden days, cookers were made of thick, robust metal and were constructed to outlive their owners. In the modern age cookers are very pretty and high-tech but they lack durability.

❏ The very expression 'consumer durable' is a contradiction in terms. The lightweight electrical products punched out by many companies are not durable at all. They are there to be consumed – again and again. The lie perpetuated by the manufacturers becomes wonderfully transparent at the very moment in time when they would prefer it not to be. Just as you are about to sign on the dotted line in Currys, the teenage assistant will ask you if you want to buy a special insurance policy to cover future repairs. When I'm confronted with this situation, the following conversation takes place:

'Why should I want to buy a repair policy? You've just told me that this product is the most reliable thing in this part of the northern hemisphere.' 'Sir, I'm afraid you don't understand. The usual guarantee expires after one year.' 'So you're saying that I'm about to spend £499 on a machine that will go wrong after thirteen months?' 'Sir, I'm not saying that at all.' 'But you're hardly filling me with confidence.' The simple truth is that the big names are not content with flogging you non-durable 'durables' – they even have the gall to try and sell you expensive insurance. The only reliable feature of most electrical goods these days is the built-in obsolescence. The commission-driven salesperson, desperate to sell the insurance, might even admit this if pushed.

❏ When compared to golden calves, consumer durables have two other very unattractive features, never mentioned by those that make them. First, their resale value is negligible. If you decide to upgrade your washing machine after three years, you may recover fifty quid or so for your old one if you sell the blasted thing through your local paper, but often it's hardly worth the effort. Secondly, dead white goods are a complete pain to throw away. Unless you are the proud owner of a Volvo estate or a Ford Transit, a defunct washing machine in your kitchen is about as much use as a tombstone. You either have to bung the dustbin men ten quid to have it removed or alternatively you get sucked further into the purchasing vortex by buying a particularly super new machine where they take away your old one 'for free'. The melt-down value of golden calves means that they are treated somewhat differently.

❏ Finally, the only thing that comes free with consumer durables is a guilt complex. Occasionally I pause and think about the terrifying amounts of now rusting metal that have passed through my hands and I pray that someone somewhere is recycling the stuff. If not, there must a vast pit somewhere overflowing with more washing-machine parts than there are stars in the Milky Way.

What Can You Do to Get Your Own Back?

Consumer durables are, by their nature, as dull as ditchwater as a topic of conversation. There is nothing special or exciting about pursuing consumer-durable complaints although the following tactics are worthy of note:

❏ If your electrical appliance has given up the ghost after six weeks you should either post it to the head office of the company who sold it to you or, if you can be bothered (which I generally can't), you should dump it at the shop. In the case of, say, a washing machine, its mere size can be a useful weapon. If, without warning, you return the offending washing machine to the store and plonk it next to the entrance, you will attract attention. Stores hate people who aggressively assert their grievances in public. The shop assistants may try to discuss the problem with you and attempt to fob you off with something less than an immediate refund or replacement. Remember that whatever else happens you do not want to waste your life negotiating with a minion. If a 'discussion' ensues, leave the electrical junk on the counter and walk away leaving the store with the hot potato. When you then write your venomous missive to the Chairman you should make it clear that his company is sitting on the goods and that you are out of pocket.

❏ Never be palmed off with the promise of repairs. A refund or replacement should always be your objective. You need a vacuum cleaner for the next six weeks. It is not good enough if your new one breaks down and the shop tries to be 'charitable' by offering to have it repaired 'free of charge'. If the rotten thing was a dud, you want a new one or your filthy lucre back. Once you are locked into repair mode, you have to start worrying about all sorts of things: badgering for the return of the goods; checking that the repair has been properly carried out; being at home for delivery; and thinking that the jinxed machine was probably built last thing on a Friday and will doubtless develop a new fault within days.

❏ Never worry about the packaging. If you've thrown away the cardboard box (the wholesale value of which is probably a few pence) it doesn't matter. This does not strip away your legal rights. When you return the duff machine, nine times out of ten you will encounter the same old stupid question: 'Where's the box? Oooh, you should have kept the box. If you haven't got the box I really can't help you.' Your reply to this should be: 'When I bought the thing I threw away the box. Why? Because I thought it was a working thing not a broken one. If I stored every box that I'd ever acquired I could set up a cardboard city in my back garden and invite Britain's homeless along for a nice kip.'

❏ The other thing that manufacturers love to baffle the public with is guarantees. Guarantees are created by manufacturers to convince the public that their goods are good goods. These documents are all too often surrounded by a strange mystique which many consumers fail to understand. It is a myth that you can't complain about goods because they are no longer 'under guarantee'. For starters, you may have a legally sound complaint based on a latent defect that has nothing to do with the manufacturer's artificial guarantee period. In any event, leaving the law to one side, there is nothing to stop you complaining if you simply feel morally aggrieved. Some companies pretend that they are doing you a favour by taking the goods back after two weeks because, lucky for you, they are still under guarantee. This is palpable nonsense. Keep the guarantee as added ammunition but don't get sidetracked by it.

❑ One of the most irritating aspects of buying consumer durables has to be the brainpower and experience of the shop assistants who sell them. If you go into a store and ask for some help from 'Dave' (his badge makes this clear) you may strike lucky if Dave is not too busy chatting up Charlotte who works on the till. You may even be fortunate enough to receive a smile and a proactive offer of assistance. As soon as you pose a difficult question, however, you will realise that there is a problem. If you ask about the power of the vacuum cleaner's engine or the durability of replacement filters you will rapidly discover that you might just as well be asking about the moon's circumference or the chemical structure of polystyrene. It's as though they have all been instructed by the companies' lawyers to say nothing. In truth, they know nothing and therefore such instructions are unnecessary. The moral of the tale is to ignore completely anything that is said to you at the point of purchase. Prevention is better than cure and you should never think that the salesperson knows what he or she is talking about. Electrical superstores pile it high and sell it cheap. Nobody knows how the stuff works, so don't kid yourself that they do.

❏ My last piece of advice on this subject is obvious but often ignored. Do not attempt to repair the rotten tumble-dryer yourself. First, there is no point in you wasting your life, however handy you might be, sorting out the problem created by the company that sold or made the sodding heap. Go and play golf or take a walk in the park instead. Secondly, if you are like me, any attempt to deal with electricity is a sure-fire route to an ugly premature death. The thought of dying with bloodshot eyes and sticking-up hair is especially unappealing. Thirdly, by fiddling around with complicated kit you will immediately give the offending company an excuse not to help you. Do not provide them with such a golden opportunity.

What Kind of Results Can You Expect?

COMPLAINT	POSSIBLE RESULT
Personal injury or damage to other goods	Decent financial compensation – manufacturers worry about something called the Consumer Protection Act 1987
Damaged goods	A total refund
Goods not to your taste	Most shops will do the M&S thing and replace unused goods returned with a receipt
Faulty goods or goods not fit for their designated purpose	A full refund – do not accept an offer to repair the goods free
A long catalogue of disastrous to-ings and fro-ings	A refund plus vouchers in respect of inconvenience

Sample Letters

You can make your point forcefully without using foul language.

Eric Ireland
Managing Director
Smeg UK Limited
Corinthian Court
87a Milton Park
Abingdon
Oxon OX14 4RY

Dear Eric

Re: Not Good Enough

I am the *Express* newspaper's Official Complainer and I write on behalf of Mrs Bond of Horfield, Bristol.

Mrs Bond has a Smeg Oven which is, to put it bluntly, smegging awful.

As your company has already acknowledged, it emits nasty and dangerous fumes which Mrs Bond and her family are not prepared to tolerate a moment longer. Her attempts to communicate with your company led to stonewalls: unanswered phone calls and incompetence seem to be the order of the day. Mrs Bond is smegging sick of the entire affair and now looks to you to smeg into

---

99

action and bring this unhappy story to a conclusion.

The fume problem comes on top of other problems. Enough is enough. Please take remedial action forthwith. I look forward to hearing from you.

Yours sincerely

Jasper Griegson

Smeg's technicians inspected the machine on several occasions, only to report that it was working normally. Nevertheless, the Smeg Customer Services Manager offered to exchange Mrs Bond's oven for a similar but more expensive model.

If the company's behaviour stinks, tell them.

Robert Allcock
Chief Executive
Parker Knoll
PO Box 30
West End Road
High Wycombe
Bucks HP11 2QD

Dear Robert

I am the *Express* newspaper's Official Complainer and I write on behalf of Arnold Worrell of Cottingham, East Yorkshire.

Arnold thought his living room would gain a touch of flair,
So he went out and bought himself a brand new comfy chair.
He wandered off to Charterlands, a sizeable shop in Hull,
And bought himself a super throne produced by Parker Knoll.

There's nowt wrong with its padding and its looks and feel are swell,
The problem is the chair emits a nasty pungent smell.
The stench is so obnoxious Arnold fumigates his room,
Or sprays the air with bucketloads of his wife's Chanel perfume.

*Although he'd like to lounge around and watch a bit of
    telly,*
*Poor Arnold can't because the chair is so peculiarly
    smelly.*
When buying the thing Arnold didn't think,
That he'd acquire a vile stink.

The wafts of musty odour are making Arnold ill,
*So I trust that now you've read this rhyme you'll surely
    find the will,*
To sort this out because it really isn't very funny,
And make your loyal customer a truly happy bunny.

I hope that your solution will make you smell of roses,
*And let poor Arnold and his wife take the pegs off from
    their noses.*

Yours sincerely

Jasper Griegson

**Parker Knoll sprang into action, launching a
thorough investigation within days, but shortly
afterwards Mr Worrell withdrew his complaint.**

It does no harm to appeal for a harmonious conclusion to the problem.

M. Wilson Esq
Commercial Director
Mamas & Papas Ltd
Colne Bridge Road
Huddersfield
West Yorkshire
HD5 0RH

Dear Mr Wilson

I am the *Express* newspaper's Official Complainer and I am a great fan of Mamas & Papas. I say this for two reasons. First, we have a Mamas and Papas pram for my recently born son Joe. We are delighted with it. Secondly, and somewhat irrelevantly, my favourite hit of the Sixties was *California Dreamin'* by The Mamas and the Papas, which you doubtless recall.

Elizabeth Jamieson of Fife is a mama who does not share my view of your company, as you will see from her attached letter. A year ago she spent £407 on the Beelzebub of all perambulators – a device so plagued with problems that if it were human, it would be lying in intensive care at this very moment. Dodgy wheels, a dodgy mudguard, a hood which fell to bits, a collapsed seating unit and an ill-fitting cover are surely not the by-products of safe and reliable workmanship.

Elizabeth is not dreamin' of California but is dreamin' of a fully working and 100 % perfect pram. I would be grateful if you would now lend some substance to this extremely reasonable expectation.

I await your urgent reply.

Yours sincerely

Jasper Griegson

Mamas & Papas' Commercial Director opened his reply to my letter by admitting that 'the prose though not the contents therein produced a wry smile or two'. He then went on to apologise for Mrs Jamieson's dodgy pram and promised to restore it 'to the best of health with the minimum of delay'.

Very often a letter to the Managing Director will receive a response from none less than the Managing Director.

Graham White
Managing Director
General Domestic Appliances Ltd
Morley Way
Peterborough PE2 9JB

Dear Graham

I write on behalf of Mr G. S. Cator.

Mr Cator bought a Cannon Cooker,
A faulty metal heap,
The most irritating bit of which,
Is its nasty random bleep.
The timer in the rotten thing,
Needs to be replaced,
The useless piece of gadgetry,
Is electronic waste.
For Cannon to carry out the work,
And for Mr Cator to be rid,
Will set him back the princely sum,
Of more than seventy quid.
Please demonstrate that you're the boss,
By sorting this out as soon as poss!

Yours sincerely

Jasper Griegson

General Domestic Appliances replaced the faulty timer and refunded the fee paid by Mr Cator.

A dramatic letter is an attention–grabbing letter.

Roger Murphy
General Manager
Braun UK
PO Box 797
Croydon
Surrey
CR9 1XF

Dear Roger

I am the *Express* newspaper's Complainer and I write on behalf of Roy Kendling of Crackington Haven, Cornwall.

In 1961 a London man woke up in the middle of the night and began sleepwalking. He was a habitual sleepwalker. On this occasion he went to his garden shed, picked up an axe, returned to his bedroom and unwittingly chopped up his wife, turning her into a messy array of uncooked quarter pounders. The moral of the tale is that accidents will happen.

Roy is the proud owner of a Braun food processor. As I understand it, the device does to chuck steak what Hannibal Lecter does to human livers. In order to protect his family, Roy would like to buy the blade cover that he noticed on the display model of the machine prior to buying it. He asks for nothing but a single sheath, a scabbard for his ruthless sword. You declined his request on the grounds that the protective thingymajigs are only available for shop use.

I have no doubt that once in a millennium your customer services department is capable of adopting a non-jobsworth approach to such matters. Please see if you can explore the possibility of sending Roy a blade cover before it is too late. Roy is a light sleeper and it would be most unfortunate if he were to wake up one night and attempt to convert his family into a smooth but full-flavoured pâté.

Yours sincerely

Jasper Griegson

Braun provided Mr Kendling with the blade cover without delay.

The disappointment of a child at Christmas is worth its weight in gold.

Beverley Hodson
Managing Director
WH Smith Ltd
Green Bridge Road
Swindon
Wilts SN3 3LD

Dear Ms Hodson

I am the *Express* newspaper's Official Complainer and I write on behalf of Faith Edmunds of London.

On 23rd December 1998 Faith used up her Christmas savings at your store in High Holborn, London WC2. She spent £19.99 on a Playstation game, 'Die Hard Trilogy'. I enclose a copy of the receipt and the empty box. Note the following word:

EMPTY

When Faith was wrapping the present for her son on Christmas Eve she noticed that it suffered from the following defects. It did not exist. Imagine her horror at the prospect of giving her son nothing more than fresh air for a Christmas present. It was obviously too late to take drastic action as all the shops were closed by this time and

Father Christmas was uncontactable (either by fax or e-mail). Faith's faith in your company emulates the game itself: she is a Die Hard WH Smith's fan. Please ensure that her confidence is justified by taking action with the kind of urgency inspired by the hero himself, Bruce Willis.

Faith and I look forward to hearing from you.

Yours sincerely

Jasper Griegson

WH Smith's Managing Director of Customer Relations got on the case and arranged for Faith Edmunds to be compensated handsomely for the disappointment she and her son had experienced. Along with the Die Hard Trilogy, two other Playstation games and gift vouchers for £10 were dispatched to them.

7
Rev It Up

(Cars)

Men and cars make for a strange mix. A dangerously high proportion of men adore their BMWs more than their wives. A polished convertible doesn't answer back, it boosts the male ego and, if its bodywork deteriorates, the old one can always be replaced by a new and better one. The fact that it guzzles money endlessly, pollutes the environment and in some cases is little more than a poor substitute for a penile extension is effortlessly forgiven and forgotten. For the male of the species, the car is an object of desire. The most coveted car is, of course, the one just outside your price range.

For women, cars take on a very different role. The car is a metal box which transports its passengers from A to B. Forget the walnut dash or the alloy wheels. Forget the in-car entertainment or the clever-dick self-adjusting air conditioning. If the car breaks down it is a bad car. If it never breaks down it is a good car. As far as women are concerned, a reliable car (like a reliable man) is the only one worth having.

What Goes Wrong with Cars?

Whatever the reason is for rational human beings becoming emotionally attached to an internal-combustion engine and four comfy chairs, the sad truth is that motorists are all too often destined to suffer severe disappointment. Cars go wrong. Motorists get upset. Why?

❏ The first problem stems from advertising. The adverts portray motoring as some form of surreal sport engaged in by well-groomed men in polished silver cars which purr their way around empty Scottish lanes. This immediately puts the motor vehicle on a pedestal from which it is almost bound to tumble. The imagery and the reality are very different. If you are stuck slap in the middle of a gridlock on the M25, your sexy new fuel-injected turbo is about as much use as a red-and-white scarf to a Tottenham supporter.

❏ Cars are made up of expensive bits. Many years ago those bits could be tampered with and played around with by a layman. The only equipment required was a brain, a spanner and strong wrists. Nowadays the bits are very expensive and all too often come in the form of sealed units that have to be replaced in their entirety if something inside packs up. This means that when things go wrong it costs a lot of money to put them right.

❏ The other thing about the bits is that there are lots of them. Given that the modern motor vehicle contains a zillion and one gizmos and gadgets it is hardly surprising that sooner or later one of them takes it upon itself to misbehave.

❏ The people who make cars make money from selling cars and selling expensive spare parts. The one activity that doesn't make them money is dealing with people like me who complain when things go wrong. Accordingly, they throw far more resources at shifting the kit on the forecourts than they do at dealing with customers' grievances. If you take your brand-new humming sports car back to the dealer, you are a nuisance. You are not a prospective purchaser, you are a prospective pain in the posterior and, however much the manager smiles, in his eyes you have metamorphosed. Don't bother kidding yourself that this is not true.

❏ Like God, cars are made in the image of man in the sense that their faults are often complex and obscure. People suffer from inexplicable aches and twinges. Cars suffer from irritating intermittent rattling noises or incorrect flashing warnings. Amazingly (as with humans), the symptoms always clear up as soon as a professional lifts up the bonnet. Even so, the symptoms tend to recur at 11.35p.m. on a dangerous unlit patch of the A4.

What Can You Do to Get Your Own Back?

There are plenty of options here, although some are more straightforward than others:

❏ Unfortunately, exhaust pipes are bigger than hamburgers. I generally advise people to post defective goods off to the Managing Director of the company concerned, but it isn't that easy or cheap to parcel up a greasy 2.3-litre diesel engine. However, this should not stop you from taking photographs of the offending hardware and passing them on to the powers that be.

❏ You may well want to make a two-pronged attack if your complaint involves a brand-new car. Write one letter to the head office of the dealer and another to the head office of the car manufacturer. Do not tell one that you are writing to the other. Get them both at it. The two heads will eventually bang themselves together but it is always a good idea to stir up as much of a hornets' nest as possible.

❏ If the problem is remotely technical, your point of view will be treated with suspicion. If enough money is involved you should invest in the opinion of a third-party expert. Ask another garage, the AA or whoever seems appropriate to express their view in writing. A damning letter from an independent professional lends your letter many times more authority than it has without such support.

❏ I have found car manufacturers notoriously difficult entities to penetrate in terms of finding out the names of the people in charge. Often, of course, the company concerned is the UK subsidiary of some monolithic foreign monster. There is no harm in writing to the President of Nissan in Tokyo or the President of Daimler–Chrysler in Detroit, but you're probably better off starting a little closer to home. Try getting the number of head office from one of the main dealers. Of course, another excellent source of information is the Internet.

❏ When you are stuck on the side of a four-lane motorway on a filthy night in November with a defective carburettor, letter-writing is not going to be of much immediate help. It is always worth joining a reputable breakdown and recovery company. Do bear in mind, however, that an RAC patrolman is not always a miracle-worker. On the contrary, anything that can go wrong will go wrong and on occasion it is not beyond the roadside repair boys to cock up.

❏ If you have bought the car from hell, you may well find that cutting your losses is your best policy. If a car breaks down eighteen times for no good reason, get rid of it. If you are forced to trade it in at a loss, that figure represents the heart of your complaint. Do not drive yourself to distraction by persisting with a car that is nothing less than jinxed.

❏ Major car complaints can involve many thousands of pounds and may not be capable of resolution by correspondence. If all else fails you may find yourself left with no option but to sue in the small claims court, which deals with disputes involving up to £5000. This is great fun but make sure you sue the dealer rather than the manufacturer. Your contract is with the former and therefore, in law, the dealer should almost certainly be the first port of call.

❑ Car problems, especially the infernal intermittent ones, require a lot more work than a gripe about a dodgy bunch of bananas. It is important to keep a careful record if the problem is persistent or protracted. The record of events should include not just the problem itself but the response by the company, especially if there are elements of indifference, rudeness or incompetence. Whatever the technical issue may be, there is no excuse for their treating you badly on a personal level.

❑ If you buy a brand–new car and discover a multitude of teething problems, do not passively accept the situation as 'one of those things'. A car is not of satisfactory quality (the legal test) just because it goes. If the ashtray drops off, the electronic side mirrors don't swivel and the windscreen wipers work only on sunny days, reject the wretched vehicle unless the dealer makes everything shipshape and gives you a decent courtesy car in the meantime.

What Kind of Results Can You Expect?

COMPLAINT	POSSIBLE RESULT
The car from hell bought new	A replacement car but this takes gritty determination and a war of attrition
The second-hand car from hell bought from a dealer	An offer of a decent trade-in if you're lucky
The second-hand car from hell bought privately	Nothing
A series of irritating teething problems with a new car	Some compensation and a decent courtesy car while the repairs are carried out
Your wife decides that she doesn't like yellow paintwork after all	Nothing

Sample Letters

When you complain, anything is possible.

Richard Parham
Managing Director
Peugeot Motor Company plc
Aldermoor House
PO Box 227
Aldermoor Lane
Coventry CV3 1LT

Dear Richard

I am the *Express* newspaper's Official Complainer
and I write on behalf Miss Joanne Watts of
Stansted, Essex.

Joanne has nothing but cutting comments to
make about her Peugeot 106 XS that she bought
from your dealer Whichfords Garage in Harlow on
1st August 1997. Why? Because ever since she has
acquired it, the car from hell has suffered from a
nasty habit: it cuts out. It does so without warning
and in potentially dangerous situations. After
umpteen fruitless visits to the garage (another
appointment has been fixed for tomorrow) Joanne is
at her wits' end. Every time she gets in the vehicle
she fears that *The Drive of Her Life* may be her last.

I would be grateful if your company would
now do some cutting out of its own: cut the crap

---

by taking some action to ensure that Joanne can drive safely and with her confidence restored.
I thank you in advance for your personal intervention in this unhappy saga.

Yours sincerely

Jasper Griegson

While Peugeot admitted no liability, they took Joanne Watts's complaint seriously enough to offer to replace her 106 XS with a new 206 XS, and organised for her dealer to supply this.

If there were ever proof needed that swearing is a bad idea, this is it.

Ken Piggott
Managing Director
Halfords Limited
Icknield Street Drive
Washford West
Redditch
Worcs B98 0DE

Dear Ken

Re: Completely ✶✶✶✶✶✶

I am the *Express* newspaper's Official Complainer and I write on behalf of Mrs C. Lelliot of Worthing, West Sussex.

As you will see, the report produced by the professionally qualified mechanic within your organisation (Mr Smith) describes Mrs Lelliot's car using the following technical language:

'Gears f★★★★d'

This blunt and somewhat uninformative diagnosis leads Mrs Lelliot to the conclusion that she has zero faith in the Service Centre concerned. She does not want to return for further free treatment. Given what I can only imagine is a bizarre departure from your usual high standards,

---

Mrs Lelliot would like a refund. If Mrs Lelliot requires abuse she can buy it elsewhere for much less than £217.00!

I would be most grateful indeed if you would demonstrate to Mrs Lelliot and our other readers that your company is totally committed to the highest standards of customer care.

I look forward to your reply which I can only imagine will use more selective words than those employed by Mr Smith!

Yours politely

Jasper Griegson

Halfords apologised abundantly for 'this lapse of good manners on the part of a member of our staff' and promised to take 'the necessary action'.

Why not perk up your letter with a Hollywood touch?

David Thursfield
Vice President
Ford Motor Company Limited
Eagle Way
Brentwood
Essex CM13 3BW

Dear David

<u>Re: The Meaning of Life</u>

I am the *Express* newspaper's Official Complainer
and I write on behalf of Ivor Baddiel and Sophie
Jubb of Muswell Hill, London N10.

Ivor and Sophie are great Ford fans. At least
they were until earlier this month when they
decided to buy a Ford Ka2 from your Finchley
Ford dealer. Their purchase has involved ineptitude
on such a cosmic scale that Ivor and Sophie are
convinced that Finchley Ford is not manned by
human beings at all. They believe that the
employees have been replaced by aliens in true
Invasion of the Bodysnatchers style. The extraterrestrial
replacements barely function in the biological sense
and if they do have brains, there is precious little
evidence of this. The problems included the
following:

- More than two hours were spent with the rep Mr Kaffel on Sunday 1st November. When Ivor rang the following Tuesday Mr K had gone on holiday and there was 'no record' of any details on the computer! Presumably these had evaporated into cyberspace or outer space or, even more vast, the space between the ears of the person in charge of the dealership.

- Tuesday to Friday was then filled with the protracted and dull regurgitation of information already handed over. Even then, the new rep, Ms Hagget, could not work out how her colleague had arrived at a monthly finance figure of £140.00. Given her limited experience (Ms H is 17) and the lack of support given to her, the problems seemed to snowball when they could have been avoided.

- On the Saturday, having just picked up the car, Ivor and Sophie had an unfortunate accident. Poor old Ms H was extremely polite and helpful but again simply couldn't cope. There was then an astronomically huge cock-up involving the arrangements for a courtesy car: Ivor and Sophie kept on being offered different cars and had to arrange and then rearrange insurance. Pandemonium was the order of the day.

- When Sophie picked up the car from the repair centre on Tuesday 17th November she encountered another wave of confusion coupled with a cocktail of indifference and, worst of all, rudeness. The centre was in a dreadful state. Two living-dead zombies kept Sophie waiting and then told her that the car was not ready (contrary to what she had been told earlier).

I know that this tale is not indicative of the standard of excellence normally experienced with Ford. The problem has its epicentre at Finchley. It may be that there is intelligent life at Finchley Ford but it is not, as Patrick Moore might put it, life as we know it. I look to you for a human response. Some time within the next Earth week will do.

Yours sincerely

Jasper Griegson

Finchley Ford's Branch Manager made amends by offering to pay for Mr Baddiel's VGI insurance and providing three years' free servicing for his vehicle.

Flatter the MD with the idea of him or her becoming the knight in shining armour by coming to the rescue.

T.W. Rhie Esq
Managing Director Daewoo Cars
Daewoo House
Homestead Road
Rickmansworth
Herts WD3 2LW

Dear Mr Rhie

I write on behalf of Mr Finlay Martin of Halesworth, Suffolk.

Let us examine the facts. Mr Martin bought a car made by your company. It burst into flames after one week. You did the gentlemanly thing and replaced it. The replacement had, also, it seems, been built on Friday afternoon by a lazy mechanic, or a robot with a grudge. That car too was so defective that you again did the gentlemanly thing and bought it back from Mr Martin. Notwithstanding all this Mr Martin is still £1200 down on the deal, having made finance payments to acquire what has transpired to be no more than fresh air!

Dig deep, Mr Rhie. In his letter to Mr Martin of 27th May 1998, your colleague Mr S. K. Kim offered nothing but a combination of hot air and, by way of compensation, more fresh air.

I have no doubt that your personal intervention will bring this unhappy story to a happy conclusion.

Yours sincerely

Jasper Griegson

In addition to expressing regret over the time it took to resolve Mr Martin's problem, Daewoo refunded his finance payments.

Remind the MD of his or her own high standards.

Norman Barber Esq
Managing Director
Charles Barber & Sons Ltd
Station Road
Northwich
Cheshire CW9 5LR

Dear Norman

What car do you drive? Whatever it is I trust that it is fairly new and that, when you drive to work in the morning, it does not cut out. If it did cut out, and continued to cut out after six visits to the garage, what would you do? Swap the car? Kill the mechanic? Take the President of the car manufacturer hostage and demand compensation?

Whatever you would do, this is the precise predicament in which Miss C. Beddard finds herself. Her Renault Clio has spent very little time on the road since she bought it last December. The garage has become her second home.

I am the *Express* newspaper's Official Complainer and I write on her behalf in the hope that you will disentangle Miss Beddard from this farcical situation. Her letter to me is enclosed.

What appears to be very striking is the way in which your company has failed to address the substance of Miss Beddard's letters, but worse, has treated her in a patronising and sometimes rude manner. Whatever happened to the maxim: The Customer is always right?

I look forward to hearing from you as a matter of urgency.

Yours sincerely

Jasper Griegson

Mr Barber wrote to me to explain that he had offered Miss Beddard the choice of another vehicle to the same value as her faulty Clio, and that she had accepted the offer 'with delight'. He also pointed out that his company had supplied Miss Beddard with a courtesy car whenever hers was being serviced and that this work was done by the local Renault main dealer.

8
Our House

(DIY and the Home)

I have never claimed to be an expert in matters such as evolution, the creation of the universe or the meaning of life. I am, however, a great believer in chaos theory. I know that if I have been asked by my wife to drill a hole in a wall, I will make a hole the wrong size, waste £7.99 on drill bits I don't need and then discover that the special Rawlplugs required for the job can only be bought from a DIY retailer based somewhere on the outskirts of Reading. Classic chaos theory dictates that everything crumbles to dust or is eventually swept away by the sea. This is very true, especially in Bournemouth on a stormy day in November.

Human beings attempt to build and create ordered things. In a Canute-like fashion they try to replace mess and disorder with neatness and beauty. This mission is as doomed to failure as Shrewsbury FC playing Manchester United with an injured striker, two players sent off and a goalkeeper with iffy contact lenses. This gloomy macrocosmic picture of the universe translates itself into an equally grim perspective when applied to a semi-detached house in suburban London. Allow me to explain. You wake up one fine Sunday morning with a view to playing a spot of golf, having a heavy lunch and then sloping off for an afternoon nap in front of a black-and-white BBC2 war film. This courageous plan is thwarted at the first hurdle by your doe-eyed spouse, who reminds you that the bookshelves that you promised to erect in February are still rotting in a heap in the garage. You take a deep breath, convince yourself that DIY is macho and head for your tool cupboard like a chocoholic confronted with an unopened box of Godiva. Although you start from a dizzy height, things will soon go wrong. Even if you are brilliant at DIY you will soon discover that: (a) the three shelves in the pack are made from seven different non-matching shades of pine; or (b) your supersonic ten-year-guaranteed German power drill produces grey-coloured nerve gas as soon as it is switched on; or (c) the tin of varnish that you planned to use is dented and has leaked on to your drill in such a way as to make the nerve gas not just deadly but smelly too.

What Goes Wrong with DIY?

Given the premise that the mere concept of attempting DIY is perilous before you begin, you might optimistically think that unimagined problems will not occur. You'd be wrong. They will. The following are classics:

❑ The mere act of going to a so-called DIY superstore is an unpleasant experience. You walk into what is little more than a vast, depressing aircraft hanger. The goods are so badly set out that you need a guide book to locate the shelf where the self-tapping 3mm brass screws are located. No one is available to assist you. After queuing for fifteen minutes at the 'Customer Service Help Desk' you eventually speak to a chinless sixteen-year-old whose vast life experience encompasses no DIY, no customers and no help. His limited intelligence makes him of little use. You search further, find the screws but then have to queue for a further fifteen minutes because the person in front of you (who has bought nine different kinds of emulsion paint, twelve roller blinds, six sacks of concrete and a shovel) has a dodgy credit card and is rowing with the girl behind the till about his non-functioning plastic.

❏ Self-assembly furniture and self-assembly kitchens are notorious nightmares. In fact, the mere expression 'self-assembly' is a watchword for grief. If you buy a dining-room cabinet that looks complete in the MFI or IKEA glossy brochure, beware. The real one, the one that you struggle to bring home in your hatchback, the one that then takes seven hours to put together, the one that looks nothing like the picture, will not be complete. The most crucial part will not only be missing but its absence will only manifest itself once you are 95 per cent through the construction process.

❏ Apart from giving you a mega-migraine when it sort of goes smoothly, DIY will give you a brain haemorrhage when it goes badly. When you discover that your new electric saw is defective, the problem will have already caused £160 worth of damage to your front door; it will be 10.30 at night and the door won't close properly; and when you finally return the wretched thing to the shop you will once again have no choice but to confront the vacuous teenager at the 'Help' desk.

❏ Because DIY is all too clearly a do-it-yourself recipe for mental anguish you might think that employing the services of 'a professional' is the answer. It isn't. When you engage an unknown builder, carpenter or handyman you wander into a whole new realm of trauma and upset. Why?

❏ The carpenter that you randomly select from the Yellow Pages will have less intellect than the two short planks from which he is supposed to build a radiator cover.

❏ He will not turn up on time and when he finally arrives will spend the first fifteen minutes talking to you about his recent vasectomy.

❏ He will not do a good job.

❏ He will demand mugs of tea by the gallon and become extremely grumpy if his throat is not regularly moistened or if you run out of Rich Tea biscuits.

❏ He will expose the upper part of his bottom when he bends down even though he is not a plumber.

❏ His oral estimate will not be worth the paper it is written on. Neither will his written one.

❏ When he comes to charge you he will move the goalposts with consummate ease.

❏ If you refuse to pay for his shoddy handiwork he will engage the services of his brother's friend, Andy the debt collector. Andy used to box for Middlesex and owns an ugly Rottweiler with a personality disorder.

What Can You Do to Get Your Own Back?

You have just moved into your new house. Whatever the estate agent said, the harsh truth is that your dream house is little more than a repossessed slum needing huge amounts of work doing to it. You are faced with the dreadful prospect of nightly DIY, incompetent builders and all-round heartache. What can you do to retain your sanity?

If you are mad enough to undertake extensive DIY work you may well find that a small, friendly DIY shop will offer the kind of help not offered by the giant superstore chains. They will speak to you, offer guidance and frequently take a more commercial approach to returned goods.

❏ Keep a very careful note of the minutiae as and when the problems start. If you are writing to the chairman of Moben to complain about the appalling condition of your state-of-the-art kitchen, it is not good enough to say that it is disgraceful and that you want the rotten thing ripped out. Equally it is not good enough to provide a thirty-page stream-of-consciousness rant in illegible spidery handwriting on lined pages torn out of an exercise book. If you attach to your letter two clear and carefully crafted schedules, this will stand you in good stead. One should set out a chronology of what happened: a description of the terrible delays and the repeated string of unfulfilled promises. The other should list the problems with a graphic account of the dire treatment you have suffered.

❏ If you are dealing with professional workmen, there is no substitute for an excellent reference. If you are forced to employ an unknown builder without a recommendation, ask him for a few referees. If he is cagey about this, you should be suspicious. You should ask him to commit as much to paper as possible. A detailed written quotation, together with a comprehensive specification, will prove to be the best form of ammunition if a row breaks out subsequently about what was agreed.

❏ If you employ builders to carry out major work, you will rarely regret spending money on a third-party professional such as a surveyor or architect to undertake a watching brief. This will be money well spent if an argument develops and you are ultimately forced to slug it out in your local county court.

What Kind of Results Can You Expect?

COMPLAINT	POSSIBLE RESULT
The widgets you bought from B&Q are defective	A full refund
Your kitchen, bought from a reputable, well-known company, is a nightmare	They'll eventually put it right and probably give you a sweetener on top
The double glazing on your conservatory develops cracks	A reputable company will go to the trouble of correcting it
Your building work (carried out by a bunch of local navvies) is dire	You'll end up in the small claims court and the company concerned will go bust

Sample Letters

Stick a rocket up the offending company.

Paul Tibble
Regional Manager
Kirkplan Kitchens
Renaissance House
176(A) Park Avenue
London NW10 7XH

Dear Paul

I am the *Express* newspaper's Official Complainer
and I write on behalf of Mrs Carole Ward of
Orpington, Kent.

I enclose for your urgent attention a picture of
a rocket. I would be grateful if you would pin it on
the wall next to your desk. Good. Now stare at it
for a minute or so and imagine that it is located
beneath your chair. Excellent. Now imagine that it
will go off unless you sort out Mrs Ward's problem
immediately. You are now in the right frame of
mind to continue.

In August of this year Mr and Mrs Ward
committed to spending £9372.00 with you in
order to obtain a spanking new kitchen. After
seven weeks of delay and with Christmas fast
approaching, it looks as though you have let them
down rather badly.

Please confirm to me by return (a) that your company will now shift into warp factor 10 and zip into supersonic action mode and (b) that your company will make a positive and meaningful gesture of goodwill to the Wards in recognition of what has happened.

Yours sincerely

Jasper 'Rocket' Griegson

Kirkplan's Customer Services Director replied promptly to reassure me that 'the delays experienced by Mr & Mrs Ward are not normal for our company' and that 'we always try to keep within an acceptable timescale'. He had already spoken to Mrs Ward and arranged for the work to be completed on Monday of the following week.

If the company has made an admission, remind them in writing.

R. Cooper Esq
Ideal Standard Limited
The Bathroom Works
National Avenue
Kingston Upon Hull
HU5 4HS

Dear Mr Cooper

Re: Less than Ideal Standards

I am the *Express* newspaper's Official Complainer and I write on behalf of Mr A. E. Lambert of Brighton.

The story in essence is this. Mr Lambert believed that by buying a complete bathroom suite built by a company with your excellent reputation, he would acquire an end product worthy of your name. What Mr Lambert has ended up with can't be likened to a beautiful proud, scarlet tulip. His bathroom is closer, in a metaphorical sense, to a hungry, rabid, carnivorous Triffid which is eating him up.

Interestingly, I have your 'Tulip' range in my house and I have had no problems at all. I can only imagine therefore that Mr Lambert's experience is extraordinary. You have recognised that his grievance is justified. Please now ensure that someone within your organisation springs into action and then produces a result which blossoms into a mutually satisfactory conclusion.

Yours fragrantly

Jasper Griegson

The problem was already in hand, according to the reply I received from the company's Customer Care Manager. It had taken too long, he conceded, but Mr Lambert was now 'totally satisfied with the solution we have proposed'. The letter ended by wishing me continuing pleasure from my own 'Ideal Standard bloom'.

A boring complaint may still be a good complaint. Keep your letter short but support it with relevant documents.

J. Kitching
Managing Director
Carpetright plc
Amberley House
New Road
Rainham
Essex RM13 8QN

Dear Mr Kitching

I am the *Express* newspaper's Official Complainer and I write on behalf of Mrs Anita Moss of Rothwell, Northamptonshire.

There are some things in life that are so good that you just want them to go on and on. I am always slightly saddened as I take the final puff of a perfect Cuban cigar or the final gulp of a magnificent claret. When watching a brilliant film like *North by Northwest* or reading a great book like *Catch 22*, I hate it when the end finally comes.

The tortuous tale of woe which Anita relates about your company is not like this. It goes on and on but it does not make compelling reading. Its protracted nature is a testimony to your company's inability to deal in a fair and caring way with a relatively uncomplicated complaint. The story, which is about as riveting as a piece of concrete, involves marks on the carpet, replacement carpet, endless fitting and refitting, a multitude of phone calls and visits from different fitters, more phone calls, problem carpet bars, and on and on and on it goes.

It cannot be beyond you to eat a huge chunk of humble pie and say: 'Sorry. On this occasion we messed up.' How refreshing it will be if you do precisely that. Make my day. Try.

I look forward to hearing from you.

Yours sincerely

Jasper Griegson

Carpetright's Managing Director apologised for the fact that 'we messed up' but was able to report that the matter had been resolved to mutual satisfaction. He ended by stressing that the company received many letters of praise and that 'thankfully Mrs Moss's case was exceptional'.

Invite the company to carry out an on–site inspection. If they refuse, this is excellent additional ammunition if you have to take the matter to the small claims court.

Andrew MacKenzie
Bryant Group plc
Cranmore House
Cranmore Boulevard
Solihull
B90 4SD

Dear Andrew

<u>Royal Flush</u>

I am the *Express* newspaper's Official Complainer and I write on behalf of Mrs P. Dormand of Knaresborough, North Yorkshire.

As King Richard III never said: 'A throne, a throne, my kingdom for a throne.'

Mrs Dormand has a problem with her throne and I would be grateful if you would resolve it. She and her husband are the proud owners of a Bryant Home. The loo at the show-home that they viewed before buying their abode was beautifully positioned. The loo at their real home is positioned in such a way that Mr Dormand cannot sit on it with any degree of comfort. I don't know if you sit 'side-saddle' on your loo but Mr Dormand has no choice

---

– his loo and the shape of his bathroom leave him no choice. One might imagine that the lay-out of the Dormands' bathroom would be a bog-standard issue if ever there was one. Sadly, this is not so.

If you do not believe Mr Dormand, he is happy for you personally to visit his toilet and carry out an on-site inspection. If you do believe Mr Dormand, please produce a truly royal result by flushing this problem away.

I look forward to hearing from you.

Yours sincerely

Jasper Griegson

Bryant Homes remeasured the Dormands' bathroom and found that the positioning of the sanitary ware fell 'within guideline tolerances and would normally be perfectly acceptable'. However, as 'a goodwill gesture', the company would reinspect the bathroom and 'implement changes that can be reasonably achieved', so that the Dormands could once again 'sit easy'.

A touch of nostalgia can prove to be a nice touch.

P.J. Talbot Esq
Managing Director
Servowarm
Stuart House
Coronation Road
High Wycombe
Bucks HP12 3TA

Dear Mr Talbot

Re: Alien Invasion

I am the *Express* newspaper's Official Complainer
and I write on behalf of Mr and Mrs Stone of
Gillingham, Kent.

Do you remember Doctor Who and the
Daleks? I found the Daleks more terrifying than
any other creatures, even the dreaded Cybermen.
You may not recall, but the Daleks were made of a
disgusting black jelly-like gunk, albeit this was
generally hidden by their polished silver exteriors.
When your company installed a new central
heating system at the Stones' home, a Dalek-like
substance escaped from the old system and spilled
its alien guts across their bedroom carpet and quilt.
It is a horrific and unsightly mess. I don't know
about you but I wouldn't fancy going to sleep with

the remains of a dead extraterrestrial. I would suggest that you call Doctor Who immediately (he tends to hang around outside a telephone box) or alternatively, agree to pay for the Stones to hire the services of another timelord–cum–cleaning contractor.

They and I await your urgent reply.

Yours sincerely

Jasper Griegson

Servowarm offered the Stones £260 'as a gesture of goodwill'.

A gentle hint at the type of compensation required can be helpful.

Martin Toogood
Managing Director
B&Q plc
Portswood House
1 Hampshire Corporate Park
Chandlers Ford
Eastleigh
Hants SO53 3YX

Dear Martin

Your secretary Suzanne Murray is a lovely lady. Please ensure that she is given a massive pay rise. Why? Because she appears to be one of the few people within your company who is able to lend a sympathetic ear when things go wrong. Moreover she is able to use the word 'sorry'.

I write on behalf of Mrs J. S. Murray-Hawkes of Wimbledon, London.

With the exception of sweet Suzanne, no one at B&Q has ever apologised for the fact that B&Q delivered a mismatching bathroom suite. Working in poor light, the mistake was not obvious to anyone until after the suite had been fitted. After enduring lorry-loads of stress and anxiety Mrs Murray-Hawkes has finally had to put up with second best: a champagne-coloured bathroom rather than the brilliant white one she ordered. Champagne should not on this occasion be associated with any kind of celebration! On the contrary, B&Q's cock-up and worse, its rudeness, should be a cause for grave concern. Your store's callous indifference was breathtaking. You personally may wish to call Mr Selwood and Mr Steer.

It would seem that Mrs Murray-Hawkes deserves a medal for patience and, at the very least, appropriate compensation: a case of bubbly would be a good start.

I trust that your customary zeal will put this saga to bed before I can say the words Moët et Chandon.

Yours sincerely

Jasper Griegson

Mr Toogood had 'no hesitation' in sending a cheque for £300 to Mrs Murray-Hawkes 'to conclude the situation to her satisfaction'.

9
Hanging on the Telephone

(Communications)

The most appropriately named inventor in history was Alexander Graham Bell. His lesser-known inventions, the electric walking stick and the inflatable budgerigar, were every bit as irritating as the telephone but ultimately proved to be less popular. Years after creating his tour de force he moved to Canada to concentrate on some other inventions. He recorded in his diary of the time that he found it difficult to concentrate because of the constant ringing of telephones! I draw some comfort from the fact that Mr Bell himself suffered from the same problem that plagues anyone who lives in the modern age: when someone wants to telephone you, you can run but you can't hide.

What Is Wrong with the Telephone Companies?

Everyone relies on the telephone for one or more areas of their life and most will have a tale of woe to tell. But what are the most common problems with telecommunications in this country?

❏ The most fundamental problem stems from the companies in power. They don't care, and BT is amongst the worst offenders. Despite having its veneer radically overhauled since privatisation in 1984, its substance seems remarkably similar to that of its state-owned predecessor. BT remains an impenetrable, amorphous monster that seems to spend mountains of money on advertising but nowhere near enough on maintaining a proper service. A few months ago the telephones in my office ceased working for no apparent reason. Trying to establish contact with someone in power was about as easy as trying to book an audience with the Pope. I was shunted from pillar to post, dialling endless numbers that seemed programmed to do little more than pass the buck. Full of optimism, you get through quite quickly to the Engineers' Department but you are not put through to a human. Instead you hear a digitally synthesised recording of someone who sounds like a female Dalek with a throat infection. It's the same experience as trying to deal with bank staff, only worse: 'If you would like to speak to our Sales Department, press 1. If you would like to hear another recorded message leading you hopelessly deeper into the telephonic labyrinth, press 2. If you would like to wait on line whilst we charge you a premium rate of 42p per minute for very little, press 3. If you would like to speak to a helpful operator who will respond swiftly to your complaint, don't bother. No one like that works for the company.'

❑ The problems associated with telephones are made all the more difficult by the jargon. You will be told when you complain that there is 'a problem at the switch'. In the mind of a non-technical person like me, a reference to 'the switch' conjures up images of a huge white knob next to a huge white socket that turns on a huge bright light bulb the size of Jupiter somewhere at BT's head office. Because you and I have no idea what a switch looks like or indeed what a switch is, it is hard to conduct a sensible discussion. You could ask BT to (a) change the fuse or (b) get a new switch, but neither of these suggestions tends to cut much ice.

❑ The other classic response is 'there's a problem at the exchange'. Do they mean a change-your-sterling-for-guilders kind of exchange? No. Or do they mean a take-it-back-to-Marks & Spencer-because-it's-the-wrong-size kind of exchange? No. They mean a nebulous, intangible spot in cyberspace from which faults on the line miraculously appear and into which telephone engineers disappear. The jargon and the concepts are so difficult to grapple with that it is extremely difficult to do battle. The telecoms playing field is not a level one.

❑ What about mobile phones? The wonders of the new technology are more than matched by the associated problems. For starters there is a weighty body of opinion that says using a mobile phone is not dissimilar to microwaving your brain. If that's true, my grey matter is probably not grey at all but more likely a well-done shade of roast-beef brown. I'm trying to cut down. Presumably, however, the Porsche-driving yuppies of the eighties (who, as you will recall, used to sport phones the size of breeze blocks) were doing for their mental agility what bread and butter pudding does for health and fitness. No wonder the fun ended with Black Monday.

❏ Cerebral degeneration aside, mobile phones are bad for you in other ways too. Mine is the size of a Mars bar and therefore constantly reminds me that I crave chocolate even when I don't. Eventually I succumb and buy half a pound of Cadbury's Dairy Milk. Telephony is thus fattening.

Of the more humdrum complaints about mobile phones the following are typical:

❏ They don't work when and where you most need them.

❏ The small print in the contract you sign at the outset proves nut-crushingly painful if you decide to terminate the wretched deal.

❏ Their Customer Services departments and helplines are more akin to brick walls (good for banging your head against but little else).

❏ The sexy deals and sexy rates are so complicated that you need a degree in mathematics and computer science to comprehend them.

❏ The batteries only ever last half the time advertised.

What Can You Do to Get Your Own Back?

❏ More than ever, it is important to write rather than phone. Despite the fact that phone companies are awash with phones, they never bother answering them. They prefer to either test out robotic answering devices or simply not bother.

❏ Keep the boring empirical evidence for use when it comes to a complex dust-up. If you want to demonstrate the fact that you keep getting charged for two-hour calls to Fiji that have nothing to do with you, you will need to keep your statements. The tedious task of keeping tidy records of dull pieces of paper is boring as hell but critical if you want to make your point. When you send your letter, attach copies of statements and any other relevant documents that might assist your case.

❏ Be prepared to enter into a flexible negotiation for compensation. The mobile phone companies in particular can offer you all sorts of things that are no skin off their noses: free air time, free accessories, an upgraded phone or a better overall deal. Often it is better to suggest these things rather than money. Money is more expensive to give away.

❏ Do not tolerate bad performance just because your phone is at the forefront of technology. Even if it is smaller than a dog biscuit the wretched thing should work properly. If it doesn't, it's because the phone company is selling a duff product.

❏ The scattergun approach to complaining is often called for. If you bought the thing from Dixons and the contract is with Orange and it doesn't work, complain to Dixons *and* Orange. If you've produced a masterpiece letter of complaint once, make it work harder for you by printing off an extra copy directed to someone else.

What Kind of Results Can You Expect?

COMPLAINT	POSSIBLE RESULT
Your statement is incorrect	They will eventually get it right but prepare for a struggle
The phone won't work	An immediate replacement is what you want – nothing less will do
Your BT phone line fails for three days	You will receive very modest statutory compensation
You enter a protracted nightmare with a mobile phone company – after four months they resolve it	Mobile phone companies can easily give away free minutes as well as financial compensation and often will

Sample Letters
Don't deal with the monkey. Go to the organ-grinder.

Richard Branson
Virgin
120 Campden Hill Road
London W8 7AR

Dear Richard

Re: The Bells! The Bells!

I write on behalf of Mr George of London NW11.
    Like the Hunchback of Notre Dame,
Mr George is plagued by the incessant ringing of
bells. The bells are not the false imaginings of a
heat-oppress'd brain. They are not a make-believe
tintinnabulation nor are they the symptom of a
rare tropical ear infection. The sound which
Mr George keeps hearing is the sound of his
telephone, which, owing to forces far beyond his
control, rings with horrendous frequency, often in
the middle of the night.
    You are to blame.
    Due to some bizarre interference in the outer
reaches of cyberspace, Mr George's telephone
number has become hooked into the Virgin
Internet Service. The Net result (pun intended) is
that every anorak on this side of the planet Saturn

who uses your Internet facility ends up calling
Mr George's phone number. Mr George is sick to
death of unsolicited telephonic garbage being
hurled by nerds in his direction.

When he complained, Virgin offered the
following solution to the problem: 'Why don't you
change your telephone number, luv?'

Brilliant. Given that he is an unwilling pawn
in a nutty game of cyber-chess, Mr George has no
intention of complying with this outrageous
suggestion. Furthermore, he has had the same
telephone number since 1945! Please speak to your
IT Department, involve Bill Gates if you need to,
sack a couple of technicians but whatever else you
do, stop the bells!

Yours sincerely

Jasper Griegson

**Virgin Net's Press Officer wrote to tell me that a
new dial-up number was being distributed to
users of its Internet service, although inevitably
some discs with the old number were still in
circulation. To overcome this problem, she
explained, all subscribers were being made aware
that they should always use the prefix, since
omitting it was what put them through to a
private number – poor Mr George's.**

Time is money. Remind the company to which you are writing that your time is as valuable as anyone else's.

Hans Snook Esq
Managing Director
Orange Personal Communications Services Ltd
PO Box 10
Patchway
Bristol
BS32 4BQ

Dear Hans

I look to you for a *Hans on* approach to a problem generated by those below you.

I am the *Express* newspaper's Official Complainer and I write on behalf of Patricia Bloomfield of Northwood, Middlesex.

As you will see, when Mrs Bloomfield hears the word Orange she sees red.

The problem in a nutshell is that Mrs Bloomfield has been robbed of 540 minutes of talktime in the course of changing mobile phone plans. She wants them back. Imagine if you had nine hours of your life snatched away from you. It's time enough to:

play six matches of football *or*

watch all the episodes of *Fawlty Towers* (with time to spare) *or*

---

roast six chickens in succession *or*
complete the marathon at a snail's pace.

Given the poor quality of the treatment that Mrs Bloomfield has received and her particular circumstances I feel sure that you can introduce a new spectrum of happiness into Mrs Bloomfield's view of your company.

I look forward to hearing from you.

Yours sincerely

Jasper Griegson

Orange's Group Director of Customer Services spoke to Mrs Bloomfield and 'resolved the outstanding issues to her satisfaction'. His letter to me emphasised that the company had also taken steps to remind all its staff of 'the importance of putting our customers first at all times' and that 'We will be using this case as an illustration'.

Getting through to BT is difficult but possible.

Michael Heffer Esq
Group Managing Director
British Telecom plc
81 Newgate Street
London EC1A 7AJ

Dear Michael

I am the *Express* newspaper's Official Complainer and I write on behalf of Mr Richard Dawood of London SW7.

Try calling his number.

It makes a nice ringing sound, doesn't it? The problem is that Mr Dawood cannot hear it. He is not deaf. He has not done a double whammy Van Gogh on himself. He has no need of a hearing aid. The problem in short is that the bell on his phone has not rung since 9th July and is not expected to ring until 3rd August at the earliest! Mr Dawood's perfect hearing seems to contrast somewhat starkly with that of your engineers, whose ears seem impervious to Mr Dawood's cries of anguish. Please exercise your quasimodo powers and make Mr Dawood's bell ring out loud and clear immediately.

The problem goes deeper. Mr Dawood cannot phone out either! Worse still, you have been charging him since 21st April for a dead line (originally linked to a burglar alarm) which your boys ripped out; a rip-out combined with a rip-off, as it were.

A grovelling computer-generated apology will not suffice. Please zap into compensation mode and demonstrate to Mr Dawood and our readers that your company takes customer care seriously.

I look forward to hearing from you.

Yours sincerely

Jasper Griegson

BT's Head of External Communications regretted the delay in providing the extra line, but said that this had eventually been connected the previous week. The company did compensate Mr Dawood – after a battle.

10
Let Me Entertain You

(Media)

George Orwell was right. Big brother really is watching you. Wherever you go in built-up areas you are never more than twenty metres away from a television, a radio, a computer screen or worse, a closed-circuit TV camera with its lens trained on you. Every day our senses take a severe battering from the media. If we have managed to evade the clutches of such quiet introverts as Chris Evans or Denise Van Outen, we find ourselves bombarded by other opinions, adverts and comments in magazines and newspapers. The scope for being entertained or informed is now so great that it is all becoming a bit too much for the brain capacity of ordinary people. I like history but I feel no need to subscribe to the Discovery Channel. I am a football devotee but I find the seventy-seven Internet sites giving up-to-date information about the latest Premiership fixtures nothing short of a complete turn-off.

That said, I am, like everyone else, a media junky. I can't drive my car without listening to the radio. I find it impossible to sit on a train without having some reading material at my disposal. I need my fix of information and entertainment whenever I want and without it I feel deprived. I scream like a baby deprived of his milk bottle if my metaphorical thirst is not quenched. It is very sad to see, for example, how much I will pay for yesterday's English newspaper when I find myself 3000 miles from these shores.

I couple together with the media, the world of entertainment generally. We are the willing recipients of stuff chucked at us by cinemas, theatres and concert halls, all of which form part of the conspiracy. If you haven't read the book or seen the film you feel an outcast and somehow you always get lured into at least buying the T-shirt.

The problem with the media and the world of entertainment generally is that lots of things are awful and the simple solution is to avoid the elements that you don't like. If ITV screen a quiz show that you despise or if the latest Tom Cruise film is dire it's not personal. They're out to poison everyone, not just you. It is very hard to complain effectively if you are doing so on behalf of the entirety of the world's population. At law you can complain about services that fail to meet the statutory test set out in the Supply of Goods and Services Act 1982: they must be of *satisfactory* quality. Although this may entitle you to compensation if your clumsy furniture removal man drops your priceless china, it does not entitle you to a ticket refund just because you went to White Hart Lane and Spurs lost 4–0 to Bradford at home. Apart from the fact that Alan Sugar sometimes seems to have had his sense of humour surgically removed, Tottenham's lawyers know their onions, so to speak. You won't get your money back just because Ginola played badly.

Complaining about the bigger issues has a cathartic benefit, particularly if you have a social conscience and a campaigning spirit, but, on the whole, your chances of success are minimal. I once complained to the BBC about the TV detective Bergerac, played by John Nettles. The complaint in essence was that I didn't like his girlfriend in the series. In my letter I described her as a whingeing, swivel-eyed old hag who would always moan just because Bergerac was called away to fight crime in Jersey in the middle of a romantic candlelit meal. I wrote to the producer of the programme requesting that the girlfriend from hell be deleted from the series. Incredibly, in the following episode, she was found murdered on a beach! It may have been a coincidence but thereafter my friends and family began to believe that I possessed magical powers of complaint.

What Is Wrong with the Media?

When does the relationship between you (the irrelevant pipsqueak) and the media moguls become personal? Let's look at some typical problems:

❏ Your night out of the month is a trip to a concert, the theatre or the cinema. The sound system is so poor that you can barely hear what is being said or sung above the ninety-decibel rustle of unfolding sweet wrappers. Your evening is spoiled.

❏ You write to a magazine to take up its special readers' offer of half-price accommodation at a hotel resort in sunny Cornwall. The magazine takes your money, cocks up the booking and leaves you to fight it out with the hotel.

❏ You enter a competition on the radio. Incredibly, you are able to name three hits by Barry Manilow. You win a prize but the goodies are never forthcoming.

❏ You believe in God and look to heaven for inspiration. You discover something called Sky Television. For reasons that have more to do with your satellite dish than divine intervention, the picture on your goggle-box looks like a fuzzy painting by Van Gogh, composed with a hangover.

❏ You love your newspaper, to which you've remained loyal for forty years, but you discover that, more frequently than ever, the TV pull-out section is missing, three pages are stapled together and page nine appears six times in a row. Believe me, these things happen. Even if you're just an occasional reader you've every right to complain.

What Can You Do to Get Your Own Back?

❏ Theatres are excellent entities to complain about. Be it an obscured view, a warm beer during the interval or a smelly tramp sitting next to you, your complaint will be taken seriously if you make it in the right way. The reason for this is that theatres don't receive

169

many complaints, perhaps because the British are too proud of their theatrical heritage. Your complaint will thus be noticed and dealt with. Again, a two-pronged attack is ideal. Do a bit of digging and find out the name of the theatre's general manager (it will often appear in the programme). At the same time write to the production company – if you couldn't sit comfortably through *The Phantom of the Opera* because a theatre barman spilled acidic tonic water all over you, don't retreat into the sewers in a huff, write to Andrew Lloyd Webber.

❏ Complaints about cinemas require similar treatment. The nice thing about cinemas is that it is no skin off their nose to shut you up with a few free tickets. In the same way that a chocolate company can easily palm me off with a few bars of the brown stuff, I am easily pacified by the thought of a free night out.

❏ If you are unhappy about something on the radio or television, feel free to cause inconvenience and hassle to some poor soul by registering your grievance with the Broadcasting Complaints Commission. By all means vent your spleen, but do be realistic: the chances of the BBC complying with your demand for Terry Wogan to be bound and gagged are limited.

❏ With the notable exception of the *Express*, of course, complaints to newspapers are difficult. If you write a letter of complaint about the newspaper to the Editor of *The Times* it is a bit like writing to the Director General of the BBC. You will receive a polite acknowledgement on a postcard spewed out by a computer and rarely more. Find someone else within the organisation to pick on. How about the Finance Director or the Head of Marketing? He or she has access to the corporate compensatory chequebook.

❏ If you subscribe to Sky or cable television you will find that you have problems. For starters you will start to have mental health problems if you overdose on daytime chat shows. More specifically, however, you will encounter 'technical' problems with the gizmo on your set or the hideous radar dish posted on the roof of your house. Alternatively, you will find that the complex array of different deals and subscription packages is a device designed to short-change you. As ever, do not duff up the TV repair man. It's not his fault. Find the name of Murdoch's henchman and write to him or her.

❏ Magazines require a two-pronged attack. If you have a complaint about *Woman's Realm* or *Top Gear* write by name to both the editor *and* someone senior at the company that owns the magazine. Don't tell the one that you've written to the other. You'll be amazed to discover how many magazines come from the same place. IPC Magazines, for example, seems to produce more publications than I've had hot dinners.

❏ Finally, you are entitled to regard the Internet as the ultimate source of entertainment, information and mirth. It is almost certain to be *the* medium of the twenty-first century. Unfortunately, however, it appears to be a headless, limbless, amorphous beast whose master is both untouchable and untraceable. Short of writing to Bill Gates, when it comes to Web complaints, your options are limited.

What Kind of Results Can You Expect?

COMPLAINT	POSSIBLE RESULT
You write to Hugh Grant complaining that his girlfriend can't act	Nothing. Not even a reply
Your night out at the theatre is spoilt by an overheated cinema	Free tickets if you're lucky
You win a non-existent prize in a magazine competition	You'll eventually get your prize and an apology
You have trouble with the installation of Sky TV	They'll sort it out ... eventually
You complain to your beloved newspaper that its editorial quality has gone to the dogs	A computer-generated acknowledgement or, in the case of the *Express*...
You are appalled at the explicit language used on a Radio 4 play and take the matter to the Broadcasting Complaints Commission (see page 255)	You will get a number of acknowledgements and eventually a rambling justification letter

Sample Letters
Loyalty deserves to be rewarded.

Bill Nicholson
Club President
Tottenham Hotspur plc
748 High Road
Tottenham
London N17 0AP

Dear Bill

I am the *Express* newspaper's Official Complainer
and I write on behalf of the son of Mrs Monica
Hylton of Palmers Green, London.

Monica's son and four friends are, like me,
devoted Spurs fans. Given their youth, however, the
boys have not, like you and I, had the pleasure of
seeing the Spurs team playing at its supreme best.
Notwithstanding the absence of Blanchflower,
Greaves and Chivers, the boys did wish to see
Spurs play in this year's Worthington Cup Final and
spent £587.50 for the honour. They were
promised seats with the Spurs supporters. Nothing
on the tickets indicated the contrary. Unfortunately
the seats were amongst the Leicester supporters and
after a short while (due to some unruly Leicester
supporters) the boys (clad in Spurs colours) were
advised to leave for their own safety.

The boys were devastated.

I would be most grateful indeed if you could demonstrate to five of Tottenham's most dedicated young fans that the Club cares about them as much as they care about the Club.

I look forward to hearing from you.

Yours sincerely

Jasper Griegson

Spurs' Finance Director discovered that the tickets had been bought from a company 'more interested in "ripping fans off"' than ensuring their safety and enjoyment', which had bought them from Leicester City, who had no record of the buyer. 'No responsibility can be attributed to Tottenham Hotspur in this matter,' he pointed out, but as an act of goodwill he offered the boys complimentary membership of the Members' Club for the following season.

Remind the institution to whom you are writing that
they are great.

R.D.V. Knight
Secretary
Marylebone Cricket Club
St John's Wood Road
London NW8 8QN

Dear Mr Knight

I am the *Express* newspaper's Official Complainer
and I write on behalf of one of our readers, Ms
Stella Bingham, who encountered an
extraordinary problem at Lord's on Friday 19th
June 1998. Stella wrote to you on 21st June but
you did not reply.

As you know, part of the joy of cricket is to
immerse oneself in the statistics. Stella takes a
particularly actuarial approach to the game,
revelling in such figures as batting averages and
bowling performances. For her, a match without
the facts and figures is akin to Christmas without a
Christmas tree, Easter without an egg or worse
still, accountancy without a calculator.

To her dismay, Stella's seat (Edrich Stand,
Lower Tier, row 10, seat 40) was a Statisticians'
Hell. The scoreboard opposite was only partially
visible (through powerful binoculars and only

when the sun wasn't shining) and the digital displays were limited to team and player scores without even naming the bowlers!

If this is the state of play at Lord's, what chance do any of us stand of preserving the grandeur and integrity of the British Empire?

Given the extraordinary circumstances of Stella's case I would be most grateful indeed if you would let me know how you might be able to convince Stella that the administration of Lord's, the MCC and British Cricket in general has not gone to the dogs.

I look forward to hearing from you.

Yours sincerely

Jasper Griegson

'A small minority of the seats at Lord's do have a restricted view of the available scoreboards,' the Secretary acknowledged, but he stated that the MCC was investing in a new scoreboard to be sited above the Allen Stand and was also 'looking at improving the level of information provided on the small digital display boards'. He very much regretted that 'on this occasion we let Ms Bingham down'.

Do not suffer in silence like the rest of the crowd. If you have a point to make, make it.

Mike Turner
Group Managing Director
British Aerospace plc
Farnborough
Hants GU14 6YU

Dear Mike

I am the *Express* newspaper's Official Complainer and I write on behalf of Kevin and Janet Gothelf. I am writing to you in the hope that your personal intervention will help resolve the Gothelfs' problem.

The Gothelfs are keen fans of high tech military aircraft. After weeks of waiting, the highlight in their annual calendar finally came to pass yesterday – a Saturday at the Farnborough Air Show. The Show had, as we all know, only one star – a single, beautifully honed diamond – the Eurofighter. The expectation grew, the crowd held its breath, the Gothelfs missed a heartbeat until…an announcement on the PA system revealed the Eurofighter would not be flying. The anodyne reason given by the announcer was that this was due to 'a technical problem'.

This isn't good enough. What if we had a 'technical problem' with four minutes to go before total annihilation by an enemy nuclear bomber? A 'technical problem' would sound like a pretty lame excuse at the post-holocaust fallout-shelter debate on the subject. Surely an aeroplane costing fifty million, squillion pounds must have been capable of taking to the air at The Mother of All Air Shows?

The long and short of it is that Kevin and Janet would very much like at least a partial refund of their £34 entrance fee. I'm sure that you could finesse this past the committee at the next Eurofighter budget meeting. Alternatively, Kevin would rather like to borrow a Eurofighter for a week or so (a working one, please!) – just to mess around with it over North London and Hertfordshire. If you've seen him drive a car you'll realise that he'd certainly put the plane through its paces.

I await your prompt response.

Yours sincerely

Jasper Griegson

Farnborough International's Director of Exhibitions & Events was himself 'desperately sorry' that the Eurofighter did not fly that day. He emphasised, however, that the Air Show's

Eurofighter was still in development and not yet in use by any air force. With such aircraft 'there are virtually no back-ups, and problems of whatever nature must be investigated under the closest scrutiny'. Furthermore, tickets for the event made it clear that the appearance of particular aircraft could not be guaranteed, and therefore no refund could be given in this case.

It's no skin off the nose of a big company to offer a freebie if things go wrong. You'll only discover this by complaining.

Anthony Portno
Chairman
Bass Leisure Entertainments Ltd
New Castle House
Castle Boulevard
Nottingham NG7 1FT

Dear Anthony

I am the *Express* newspaper's Official Complainer and I write on behalf of Karin and Dave Harrold.
　　Earlier this year Karin and Dave took the brave decision to hold a birthday party for their

eldest daughter Jessica at The Hollywood Bowl bowling centre in Watford. Karin made the booking in good time. If you have had children you will appreciate that keeping control over 25 energetic nine-year old girls requires the patience of a saint, the strength of an ox and the authority of The Lord Chief Justice. In ordinary circumstances this would have been achievable but on their arrival disaster struck.

The kids turned up on time at 4.15p.m. but at 4.30p.m. Karin was told that the bowling could not begin: insufficient lanes were available. By 5.00p.m. nothing had changed. No bowling – just rampaging kids. By this time Karin was having a nervous breakdown. Dave toyed with the idea of sneaking off to the bar for a swift pint of Bass's finest but was stopped by his conscience! There was a complete lack of information or organisation and it was 5.15p.m. when the staff finally sorted out the problem.

The knock-on effect was inevitable. The post-match munching had to be squeezed into 20 minutes. What should have been a jolly tea party became a bizarre feeding frenzy made all the more crazy due to a lack of spoons for the ice cream! Had the Mad Hatter been organising the affair he would have been proud.

Jessica's party was, in short, a shambles. I would suggest that you bowl over the Harrold family with a substantive and meaningful gesture of goodwill.

I thank you in advance for your concern and await your earliest reply.

Yours sincerely

Jasper Griegson

The Hollywood Bowl's Regional Manager invited the Harrold family to return as the company's guests and provided them with eight free game vouchers.

Even apparently dull institutions are full of real people who have a sense of humour and a regard for fairness.

Sir Christopher Bland
Chairman
British Broadcasting Corporation
Broadcasting House
Portland Place
London W1A 1AA

Dear Sir Christopher

I am the *Express* newspaper's Official Complainer and I write on behalf of Emily Lyons (aged 21 months) of Sale, Cheshire.

Has the BBC been infiltrated by the dreaded Goblins? Has the Dark Dark Wood cast a dark dark shadow over BBC Television Centre in Wood Lane? Is Noddy two-timing his fans? These questions and others need answering now.

Emily is a young girl who queued for 2 hours with her daddy at your event in Birmingham called 'The Little Bash'. She went for the sole purpose of meeting and being photographed with her bell-capped hero. After patiently waiting in line following a 200 mile journey Emily could hardly believe her little ears when she heard that Big Ears and his pal Noddy had effectively bunked off. This was revealed just as Emily approached the front of the queue! This was a situation that could easily have been avoided. As a result there were a vast number of small people (including Emily) who had their expectations falsely raised and then tearfully dashed.

When Emily wrote to the BBC your reply was no more forthcoming than Enid Blyton's next novel. No doubt you will want to make amends to Emily for her wasted journey and very unhappy day. Be warned! Failure to respond positively will result in this matter being reported to PC Plod. Incidentally, why is it that he hasn't been promoted after all these years?

Yours sincerely

Jasper Griegson

Noddy was clearly a victim of his own success, according to Sir Christopher's letter to me. Such was his popularity that, towards the end of each day, it became clear that 'not all his young (and old) friends were likely to meet him'. The Chairman invited Emily to take some consolation from the thought that 'Noddy is determined that we shall try harder next year to make everybody happy'.

11
Light My Fire

(Utilities)

When I was a child in the 1960s there were a number of great mysteries that played constantly on my mind. Why did God allow Jimmy Greaves to be dropped from playing in the World Cup Final? Why did my parents believe that if I was given a whole Mars bar all to myself I would be sick? Why did men bother getting married to women when women can't tell the difference between *Thunderbird 1* and a *Saturn V* rocket? These important matters eventually resolved themselves but one Great Mystery remained. Why were Batman's trousers-cum-underwear held up by something that he and Robin referred to as a 'utility belt'? I knew that Batman stored a series of wonderful gadgets and gizmos in feminine pouches around his paunch (a bit like a Brownie) but I never understood the 'utility' bit. I learnt later from my grandmother that during the war there existed a type of rationed clothing which bore the title 'utility' (utility vests were especially popular) but this only served to confuse me more. It was only when I started studying A-level economics that I realised 'utility' had nothing to do with belts or vests but everything to do with gas, electricity and water.

I also discovered that everything to do with the utilities is mind-numbingly dull. The empirical proof (if proof were needed) of the boredom they induce is provided by one simple test. Who in their right mind plays Monopoly and nurtures the dream of buying the Water Company and the Electricity Company? The answer is no one. These properties make the Old Kent Road look interesting. So boring are the utilities that even I struggle to write a letter of complaint when faced with an incorrect gas bill or a misread electricity meter. Halfway through the second paragraph my eyelids start to roll and before I finish the third paragraph I am curled up on the sofa taking forty winks.

This is perfectly understandable when you consider that the privately owned utilities are the unwanted love children of the defunct dinosaurs formerly known as the nationalised industries. It is not just octogenarian ladies with blue rinses who try to relive the excitement of the past by referring to Norweb plc or Southern Electricity plc as 'the Electricity Board': I understand that the same terminology is used by a die-hard minority of employees.

What Is Wrong with the Gas, Electricity and Water Industries?

There is a powerful link between the culture of the utilities and the everyday problems faced by consumers of their services.

❏ The boredom faced by the consumer is more than matched by the boredom of the people working in the industries themselves. The most exciting thing in the unhappy life of a bean-counter at Eastern Gas's Norwich office is the next episode of *EastEnders*. Life may be a gas but gas is not. Because the people who work for what used to be called the Gas Board, the Electricity Board and the Water Board are very bored indeed, things go wrong. The problems rarely concern the product. You are unlikely to know or care if your gas has changed colour or if your water pressure has risen or fallen a fraction. You do have a problem, however, if the gas company's heavies are banging on your door with a court order, waiting to cut off your supply from the North Sea. And of course you care if the electricity company decides to charge the cost of the Christmas lights in Oxford Street to your humble abode in Acacia Avenue. Customers' anger is often well founded. Mrs Goggins, a blind ninety-year-old, does not owe £6000 for two months' worth of use from her three-bar electric wall heater. Mr Stephens should not be charged for hosepipe use since the garden to his flat on the sixteenth floor of a high-rise flat consists of nothing more than a window-box.

❑ This brings us to the people who man the phones at the customer service desks. Here you run smack into another problem. Chosen for their vocal and physical resemblance to rhinos and their bomb-proof temperaments, they are there to take the flak. These hardy front-line troops have one job and one job only. They exist to form an impenetrable barrier between the outraged consumers and the people within the organisation who could solve the problems, if only they cared. Day in, day out these thick-skinned souls absorb the screams and hatred of the seething masses, soaking up anger like sponges and spitting out 'comforting' platitudes with the rapidity of a machine-gun. But where does that get the caller?

What Can You Do to Get Your Own Back?

You can't live without a regular supply of gas, electricity or water unless you are extremely fond of camping and can afford to bathe in Evian water. Accordingly, you have no choice but to deal with the monolithic powers that be who control the services you require. What should you do when things go horribly wrong?

❑ A good way to gain sympathy is to be old. The gas company will not cut you off if you might die as a result. Their accountants have calculated that they make more money out of a living person, even though they make a very fast buck out of a fry-up at the crematorium. If you are eighty it is not hard to pretend that you are old. Faking a croaking voice when you are twenty is more difficult. A few years ago my thirtysomething neighbours explained that they had a serious problem. They had received no electricity bill for five years. Suddenly the dreaded letter arrived seeking payment of thousands of pounds. What should they do? I instructed my neighbour to write a pleading letter on exercise paper addressed to 'the Electricity Board' in spidery biro with his left hand. His heart-warming tale recounted how he and his wife put aside a few coppers each week for cat food and a trip to the bingo club and how a £3000 bill was nothing short of devastating. The letter made no reference to their age. The electricity company gave a generous discount and allowed my neighbours to pay by sensible instalments. Naughty but satisfying.

❑ Because the things that utility companies do are so drab, a spot of humour will often go a long way. If you can lighten up the life of the electricity company's Finance Director (even by a flickering thirty watts or so) you may find that he or she responds well. Given that the job probably involves counting paper clips and making paper gliders from computer-generated spreadsheets, a light-hearted consumer complaint may come as welcome relief.

❑ If (as so often happens) the debt-collection boys start legal proceedings against you in the County Court (even though the sum due is £0.00), counterclaim. Seek punitive damages for conspiracy, false imprisonment and manslaughter. That tends to grab the attention of the legal department, who up until that point will have studiously ignored the fact that no money is owing. Alternatively, sue the chairman of the company personally. There is no basis in law for doing so but it certainly makes the people who matter sit up and pay attention if they haven't done so beforehand.

❏ Given that utility companies are huge, faceless monsters who blame everything on 'the computer', you should play them at their own game. Get your computer to generate a bill for £40 in respect of your misery and send it to their accounts department for payment within thirty days. After the expiry of the deadline you can then start chasing. You may never get paid as a result but it's great fun trying.

❏ If you can't beat them confuse them. If you are dissatisfied with the mathematical explanation given for your mind-bogglingly large electricity bill, start expounding your own thoughts based on differential calculus and Pythagoras's Theorem. Alternatively, cite long passages from Section 14(1) (a) of the 1991 Gas Supply Safety Regulations. They don't exist, so feel free to be verbose.

❏ A dispute in which you owe money is a dispute you never want to end. By fighting a war of attrition you will generally wear out the opposition to the point where they give up on the grounds of indifference. If a utility company engages you in correspondence demanding money which, in part only, is genuinely owing, there is nothing wrong in stringing out the complaint until the Coming of the Messiah. The longer the letter the better. The more your complaint gets passed from pillar to post by different departments the better.

❏ When you have a complaint about British Gas be careful about who you write to because British Gas, as such, does not exist. The company was split into two parts several years ago. Centrica plc seems to deal with the nasty brown envelopes that land on your doorstep and the smelly stuff that comes out of your oven. The other company, Transco (otherwise known as BG plc), seems to deal with bigger issues like mucky underground pipes and gas explosions.

❏ Since we now live in an age of competitive enlightenment you may decide to express your complaint by switching gas or electricity companies. If you do this, prepare yourself for a battle of Second World War proportions. I have seen more complaints arising from changeovers than anything else. The promise may be of lower charges but if the price involves a throbbing migraine you may well be better giving it a wide berth. Be very wary of high-pressure door-to-door salesmanship from supposedly reputable companies encouraging you to transfer. Salesmanship and morality are uncomfortable bedfellows.

❏ There is no harm in contacting the regulatory watchdogs (see page 262), whose involvement may prove useful.

What Kind of Results Can You Expect?

COMPLAINT	POSSIBLE RESULT
The gas company sends bailiffs to your house in error	An apology if you're lucky
You are billed the wrong amount	A correction but you'll be forced to prove your case beyond all reasonable doubt
The water company doesn't bill you for four years and then hits you with a quadruple whammy	A good chance to pay off the outstanding sum by instalments
Damage to your property caused by their default (a gas explosion)	Full compensation but a row about the quantum of your loss

Sample Letters

Utility companies think they have a God–given right to leave a mess when they carry out work.

Sir Robert Clarke, Chairman
Thames Water plc
14 Cavendish Place
London W1M 0NU

Dear Sir Robert

I write on behalf of Ms Elizabeth Balsom of London SW15. Last summer your company dug holes on Elizabeth's property in order to carry out some leak repairs. They filled in the holes afterwards but Elizabeth's once beautiful path is now a collage of footprints, strange ridges and curiously clashing multi-coloured concrete. A few years ago British Gas did a wonderful restoring job for Elizabeth. Why couldn't your employees behave themselves and do the same?

Yours sincerely

Jasper Griegson

Ms Balsom's garden path was reinstated courtesy of Thames Water.

If they switch you off they should be made to pay you off.

Ian Robertson
Chairman
Scottish Power plc
1 Atlantic Quay
Glasgow
G2 8SP

Dear Ian

I am the *Express* newspaper's Official Complainer and I write on behalf of Mr and Mrs G Thomson of Bannockburn, Stirling.

I don't know about you but I am quite partial to strongly flavoured meat – duck, venison and oxtail all appeal to my highly developed palate. Notwithstanding my preference for a gamey aftertaste, even I cannot bear meat that is positively mouldy. The Thomsons share this view and I am sure that you do too. Why is it then that your company has no sympathy for the Thomsons when they were faced with the choice of consuming the unconsumable or throwing it in the bin? When the freezer which they bought from your store in Stirling failed, they lost £130. You have offered them a truly rotten 20 quid, which they have rejected.

I would be most grateful if you would chew on the dilemma facing the Thomsons and spit out a positive response by return.

I look forward to hearing from you.

Yours sincerely

Jasper Griegson

Scottish Power's Customer Liaison Manager telephoned Mrs Thomson and, as a result of his enquiries, the company agreed to pay her £90 by way of compensation.

Note the mistake here. I should have written to Centrica rather than British Gas (BG). Note also that the refuge of all companies is the most common excuse of all: it was the fault of the computer. This is not acceptable.

Richard Giordano
BG plc
100 Thames Valley Park Drive
Reading
Berkshire

Dear Richard

I am the *Express* newspaper's Official Complainer and I write on behalf of Mr L. Hardy, aged 79, of Braintree.

Mr Hardy's complaint is quite remarkable and I would be grateful if you would resolve it immediately.

Mr Hardy does not use gas, has not used gas for many years and does not intend to use gas at any time in the future. Notwithstanding this spectacularly simple situation, Mr Hardy is being hounded for £79.40 by your company and is currently in receipt of a number of threatening letters.

My theory is that somewhere within your head office there is a rogue computer with a nasty streak – a bit like 'Hal', the wayward computer in

---

the film *2001 – A Space Odyssey*. Please arrange for one of your strongest and ugliest gas–pipe engineers to pay this computer a visit armed with a huge rusty spanner and a crowbar. The engineer should then be instructed to carry out some violent 'repair work' on the computer's RAM drive, thus subjecting it to the same kind of treatment as that which Mr Hardy has received.

Once the computer has had a thorough thrashing I suggest that an apology and a gesture of goodwill to Mr Hardy would be entirely appropriate.

I look forward to hearing from you.

Yours sincerely

Jasper Griegson

An apologetic letter landed on Mr Hardy's doormat confirming that the account had been closed and that no charges applied. The Customer Service Adviser also arranged a payment of £10 for his expenditure on telephone calls and letters.

12
Bring Down the Government

(Central and Local Government)

Defeatism aside, another flaw in the make-up of the British is that we are scared of authority. We are twitching rabbits who scurry away into a dark corner as soon as there is the slightest possibility of a conflict with the powers that be. Even if we summon up enough courage to pen a letter to our local supermarket, it rarely even occurs to us that we are perfectly at liberty to wage war on the government. The nearest most people get to a confrontation with Big Brother is to proclaim the following words: 'I'm going to write to my MP about that.'

This sudden impulse towards rebellion usually ends there. The combined hurdles of putting pen to paper, buying a stamp and trudging to the postbox usually prove insurmountable. It is no wonder that we haven't had a civil war here for nearly 400 years. The simple truth is that you need not be afraid. The death penalty was abolished in 1964; witches are not summarily burned at the stake and the government's power to lock you up simply because you are ugly and smell went out with the Magna Carta. The government, at local or central level, is as good a target as any for the confident and proficient complainer.

Does the government work? There are two answers to this. The first is this: of course the government doesn't work. As we all know, Cabinet ministers are far too busy undertaking extensive late-night research with their blonde graduate assistants to do any work either that night or the following morning. In short, they are shagged out. The politicians that are genuinely keen on politics are far too preoccupied with advancing their careers to worry about doing their jobs.

The second answer is this: the greatest myth about government is that it exists in the first place. It doesn't. It's largely irrelevant and the things it does are of no real concern to ordinary people living ordinary lives. Take, for example, the Acts passed by Parliament. No one in the real world knows what the law of England is because the books that make up the law would fill an aircraft hangar. In any event, most people are not fussed either way what the law says because on the whole the law makes zero impact on their everyday life. The government is not 'mother'. It is out there somewhere but most people couldn't give a tinker's cuss what it does unless it puts up the price of fags. The government, on the other hand, thinks it is very important (which it isn't) and that the earth would stop spinning without it (which it wouldn't).

On a macrocosmic scale there is nothing to stop you writing to Tony Blair. He may not agree with you that income tax should be abolished or that root beer is the root of all evil, but for the price of a first-class stamp you are quite free to vent your spleen. For the sheer catharsis of the exercise, it is sometimes worth writing to someone very powerful explaining the difficulties you are having with the bus stop that has been plonked outside your house. Even if John Prescott doesn't turn up the following day with a sledgehammer and a team of burly civil servants, you will still start to feel better about yourself.

What Is Wrong with the Government?

As anyone who has watched a Hammer horror film knows, the devil manifests himself in a multitude of different forms. One minute he's a black alley cat, the next he's a red-faced imp with horns and a trident. The government is similar. Whether your problem concerns the education system, the National Health Service, the police, the planning authorities, the Inland Revenue or your local library, it ultimately boils down to one entity: the government. The government does bad things to you for lots of different reasons but on the whole the problems tend to arise as a result of two factors: (i) incompetent, indifferent and underpaid staff; and (ii) a shortage of money. Compare and contrast, for example, a night's stay at the worst example of an NHS concrete slum with the equivalent experience at a BUPA establishment. The quality of medical care may well be similar but at the former the mashed potato will be cold and lumpy. At the latter some arty designer chef will have liquidized the spuds himself before garnishing his elegant creation with a sprig of mint. Schools are another example. If your child goes to the local state school, he or she is unlikely to get the same start in life as a child of similar ability who finds himself at Eton. Not only will the latter child become very knowledgeable and incurably assertive, but he will, by the age of eight, have made fantastic stockbroking connections. Boghill Junior School does not offer the same career prospects to a child keen to become in later life either a Russian double agent or an insider dealer. It's not fair.

What are the most common, humdrum clashes you are likely to have with the government? The following are typical.

❑ You go to your local hospital's Accident and Emergency Department after slipping on the pavement and injuring your arm. You are kept waiting for six hours before being seen.

❑ Your radio-ham neighbour is granted planning permission to erect a satellite dish the size of St Paul's in his back garden. From your perspective the ghastly construction is an offensive eyesore.

❑ You park quite legitimately in a municipal 'pay and display' car park. The sticky ticket falls off your windscreen without you knowing and you incur a £60 fine.

❑ You have a disagreement with your local tax inspector but eventually an agreement is reached whereby you pay £800. You cough up the money but two weeks later you receive a further bill for the interest on your debt.

❏ Your local authority grants permission to the Post Office to build a gaudy red postbox two yards from your front gate. The ugly obelisk is very convenient but irritatingly awkward when you are reversing your car into your drive.

What Can You Do to Get Your Own Back?

When it comes to the government, the weaponry normally available to even the most seasoned complainer does not exist. Why? First, if you pay for your hospital bed with a cheque on the spot it is very different from paying for a hospital bed via the PAYE system and the Chancellor of the Exchequer. With BUPA, you have a contract and this fact means empowerment. If BUPA were to serve you poisonous chicken salad you could refuse to pay your bill. If the NHS conspires to polish you off with salmonella you can't refuse to pay the tax man. Secondly, BUPA wants to keep you happy for commercial reasons. If it fails to deliver high-quality service you can switch your custom to another company. In the same way as there is only one Monopolies Commission, there is only one NHS. If you informed your local NHS hospital that you were taking your custom elsewhere they would not lose sleep over it.

❏ Because the public sector does not, on the whole, give a damn, you are usually left with a single blunt instrument: create a stink. If charm fails (and it usually will unless you happen to be blonde and beautiful) you must make such a fuss that, in the end, the civil servant or local librarian or whoever it is gives in. Apart from the emergency services (who are wonderful), the driving force behind many people who work in or for the government is apathy. A letter of complaint to your local tax office will never be processed quickly because it is easier for them to take three weeks rather than one to reply. You therefore have to turn the process on its head and make it easier for them to dispose of your complaint rather than process it slowly or ignore it. As with commercial enterprises, a rabid rant on the spot is of little use. The person called Colin who works behind the counter at the civic centre enquiries desk is not the person who will solve the problem with your council tax.

❏ To create a stink you must address the problem at all levels. Do not start at the bottom and go up. Start at the top and then zap everyone else in sight at the same time. Take the example of a bus stop whose annoying position on your street, for some reason, causes you offence. I would start my campaign by writing to the following people: the Secretary of State for Transport, the Chief Executive of the bus company, the Chief Executive of the Local Council and, what the hell, my local MP. This approach will put the cat among the pigeons, if nothing else. A polite telephone call to the branch office of the bus company will probably not produce the same kind of outcome. In other words, a complaint against a governmental body or agency requires carpet-bombing by correspondence. The more targets you can find to shoot at, the more likely it is that someone somewhere will do something. The he or she concerned will, when dumped upon from a great height, realise that a quiet life is best achieved by dealing with your problem.

❏ When complaining about government bodies there is no harm in adding a third party into the melting pot. A letter to the relevant Ombudsman (if a relevant one exists; see page 254) costs nothing and can help you to pile on the pressure. The Parliamentary Ombudsman, the Health Service Ombudsman, the Local Government Ombudsman and the Pensions Ombudsman are among those you might choose to approach. Do not, however, rely on these institutional watchdogs to solve your problem. They will investigate maladministration and so on, but they should not be treated like judges. Moreover, many are seriously overloaded and take for ever to deal with your complaint. As far as I know there is no ombudsman appointed to keep an eye on all the other ombudsmen.

What Kind of Results Can You Expect?

COMPLAINT	POSSIBLE RESULT
Petrol is too expensive	Nothing
You are unjustly given a parking ticket	You can extricate yourself from payment by going to the top – especially if you have any evidence (like a photo) to support your complaint
You receive brutal and uncaring treatment at the hands of an NHS nurse	A complaint against personnel will be taken very seriously by the powers that be
The taxman's mathematics are so bad that he miscalculates your tax bill by £2000 on three separate occasions. When challenged on the phone, he becomes rude	This is winnable. Follow the boring correct procedure for registering a complaint, remind them of their own code of conduct but in any event write to the Chancellor of the Exchequer
You bring a claim in your local small claims court but the court loses all the papers	You could sue the court but I wouldn't advise it. A polite written plea for compensation might do the trick

Sample Letters

Even passport problems can be sorted out if you go to
the top.

The Right Hon. Jack Straw MP
Home Secretary
House of Commons
London SW1

Dear Jack

I am the *Express* newspaper's Official Complainer
and I write on behalf of Pamela Telford of
Cumbria.

I know that you have got an awful lot on your
plate at the moment but whilst you're sipping your
morning coffee I wonder if you could sort out
Pamela's problem. I'm sure a quick phone call to
one of your mates will resolve it in a jiffy.

Pamela is a lone parent with four children.
She has struggled to save enough money to take
her family on holiday in late June. In early March
her passport disappeared into The Black Hole of
No Return, otherwise known as the Liverpool
passport office. As you know, trying to contact the
Passport Office is about as easy as trying to reach
alien life forms on the planet Zog. Pamela has tried
and failed and is now desperately worried that her
much-needed vacation will be kicked into touch

by the inefficiency of the system. Her phone calls are passed from one recorded message to another and the passport 'hotline' leaves Pamela cold.

Your personal intervention would be gratefully appreciated, especially by Pamela's kids, who are counting the days until they go away.

Yours sincerely

Jasper Griegson

Approaching the Home Secretary direct paid off. His staff contacted the Passport Agency and advised Mrs Telford to attend the Liverpool passport office in person with her application form and the necessary documents.

Local authorities can behave like the judge and jury rolled into one. Make sure that the case for the defence is properly heard.

Dorian Leatham
Chief Executive
London Borough of Hillingdon
Civic Centre
Uxbridge
UB8 1UW

Dear Dorian

I am the *Express* newspaper's Official Complainer and I write on behalf of Mrs Sue Drake.

Sue is – quite understandably – a bit disillusioned with British Justice at the moment. I wonder if you could intervene and reassure her that fair play, the rules of cricket and gentlemanly behaviour are still the cornerstones of British life.

Sue parked her car in a 'pay and display' car park. She returned well in advance of her ticket's expiry time. She is innocent. Mistakes happen and I can only imagine that the traffic warden's myopia is the true cause of this injustice.

Sue is minded to tie herself to the railings outside the council's offices until this matter is rectified. I have advised her against this (a) because

---

chains can be very uncomfortable and (b) because the council officials are probably too short-sighted to notice and (c) there are no railings outside the council's offices!

This case is a cesspit of unfairness. Please step in.

Yours sincerely

Jasper Griegson

Admitting the attendant's error, the Council waived the fine.

Cut through the red tape by going for the jugular vein of the organisation concerned.

S. Bundred Esq
Chief Executive
Camden Council
Camden Town Hall Extension
Argyle Street
London WC1H 8NG

Dear Mr Bundred

Re: A Load of Bollards

I am the *Express* newspaper's Official Complainer and I write on behalf of Ms Miller of London SW3.

Ms Miller's tale of woe is simple. At 12.30 a.m. on 25th May this year she turned right into St Mark's Square (the one in Camden, not Venice). The road was badly lit and she hit (at no more than 30mph) a redundant pedestrian island which had not been properly removed. The damage to her VW Polo totalled £950.

Your Claims Department appears to suffer from the same malaise as your Highways Department: both seem inefficient, indifferent and in a mess. Ms Miller has become inextricably entangled in a forest of bureaucratic red tape from which there would appear to be no escape. The defunct bollard has been metaphorically reincarnated in your administrative system as an obstacle to compensation. Although you failed to remove the original obstruction, how about flattening this one?

Yours sincerely

Jasper Griegson

Mr Bundred wrote saying that 'the Council has got this one wrong' and that it was now his job to find out what went wrong and to put it right for the future. More tangibly, Ms Miller received a letter of apology containing a cheque in full settlement of the sum in question.

You can't change government policy (I'm still waiting for a reply and the price of petrol continues to rise)...

Gordon Brown
Chancellor of the Exchequer
House of Commons
London SW1

Dear Gordon

As you know, I am the *Express* newspaper's Official Complainer.

Last weekend I filled up my car with petrol. It cost £50.00. I have decided that this is far too much and I would be most grateful indeed if you would reduce the tax on petrol before next weekend when I have to fill up again. The price is a shocking £3.50 per gallon (I haven't a clue what that is in euro-litres) and I am not prepared to tolerate this rip-off a moment longer. In America you can fill up your car for a tenner and still have enough change to buy a couple of Hershey bars and a box of Dunkin' Donuts.

If you decide to ignore my plea I will have a quiet word with my mate Tony. I will recommend that you be reshuffled to Junior Fuel Under Secretary in the Department of Automotive Affairs. Then you'll be sorry.

Come on Gordon, give back to British

motorists the four-star dignity they deserve and cut the price tomorrow. You know you want to.

By the way, I never did manage to get Jeff Astle for my 1970 Esso World Cup coin collection – have you got any swaps?

Best regards

Yours sincerely

Jasper Griegson

…but if the problem is personal, anything is possible.

Rt Hon John Prescott MP
House of Commons
London SW1

Dear John

I am the *Express* newspaper's Official Complainer and I write on behalf of Mr S. Collins.

I know you have a lot on your plate at the moment – keeping the traffic flowing, improving safety on the railways, checking air traffic control for the millennium and polishing the ministerial fleet. Notwithstanding these burdens of high office, I wonder if you could spare five minutes to sort out a problem drawn to my attention by Mr Collins. It affects hundreds of people in London every day, particularly during the rush hour.

What you need to do is pop up to Holborn tube, turn left out of the station, wander 50 yards or so down Kingsway and buy yourself a coffee and a cheese roll. You will then be well prepared to spend a few minutes watching all the traffic lights on the junction with Remnant Street. Don't forget to dress up warmly at this time of the year.

What's the problem? The phasing of the traffic lights is dangerously up the creek. The issue is this. If you attempt to turn right out of Remnant Street into Kingsway (in a car!) you immediately arrive at a pelican crossing. The phasing is such that the traffic lights and the pedestrian crossing lights are green at the same time. Cars therefore sail round the corner only to meet pedestrians crossing the road blissfully unaware of the oncoming vehicles. There is a serious risk that sooner or later someone will get badly injured or worse on this crossing.

Following your site inspection please speak to Colin or Doris. They are two of your most long-serving but lowly subordinates who work in the depths of the Ministry – sub-basement 3, corridor F, room 8156. You know – the department that spends hours deciding where to install all those annoying little bumps in the road where they are not really needed. Tell them to stop messing up London's traffic whilst pretending to help and do something really useful for once.

Provided you sort this out I promise to endorse you as a candidate for one of the most sought after transport positions this side of Neasden: Honorary President of The Tufty Club (London Division, Holborn Branch).

Yours sincerely

Jasper Griegson

Within two months of my letter the phasing of the traffic lights was changed, improving safety for all at this hazardous spot.

13
My Top Thirty-nine Tips

1. Commit your complaint to paper. If you have a complaint that can't be resolved on the spot do not lose your temper, bang your fist on the counter and then rant and rave at the lowly shop assistant. Revenge is a dish best enjoyed cold and you will do far better to go home and compose a carefully worded letter that sets out your problem clearly and concisely. A good complainer's objective is not to get mad but to get even, and the best way of doing this is in writing. The pen is more powerful than the sword.

2. If you are aggrieved you should treat no wrong as too small to warrant a complaint. If you feel like registering a complaint, get it off your chest, get it on to a piece of paper and get it into a postbox. Do not bottle up your anger. Do I practise what I preach? My smallest complaint ever concerned an ant. London Zoo operates a scheme whereby you can adopt an animal for an annual fee. You get a photograph of the beast and a certificate. Elephants are very expensive, so as an appropriate present for a tight-fisted relative I decided to adopt the cheapest

creature available: a wood ant, priced at £15. Imagine my horror when I received a certificate for the wrong kind of ant: a soldier ant. Did I bother to complain? Can Delia cook?

3. A good complainer is a happy complainer. If you are uncontrollably angry you are unlikely to write a good letter of complaint. Before committing yourself to paper, wait a while, make yourself a cup of tea, compose yourself and *then* compose your letter. You will be surprised how often a cheerful, even humorous, letter will achieve a far better result than a vitriolic tirade. It is worth remembering at all times that large reputable companies want to keep you as a loyal customer and will generally respond positively to a positively written letter. It is usually a good idea to mention how your devout loyalty has been shaken by this one extraordinary incident. The last thing you should ever write is: 'I'm never shopping with you again.' Give the company concerned a chance to win you back.

4. Sometimes it is necessary to fight a full-blooded war of attrition. Just because your first letter meets with a rebuff there is no reason why you should not (a) challenge the points made in response; (b) write to another main-board director for a second opinion; (c) involve a third party such as Trading Standards or an official watchdog; or (d) continue

corresponding until the company gets so sick of you that it finally surrenders. If you remain cool, polite and determined, the fruits of your efforts will often emerge from the most protracted of disputes.

5. I am frequently asked how to locate a particular company's head office. There are a number of ways. The head office's address often appears in small print on documentation you might ordinarily ignore – tickets, menus, term and conditions and brochures. A local branch office is always a good bet – ring up the Orpington office of Bloggs & Co and ask them for the particulars of their HQ. Other rich veins of information are the Internet and directories (available in your local library). If all else fails, for a small fee Companies House (the official source of all company information) will supply details by post or fax.

6. *Carpe diem*. It is not often that I dish out advice in Latin but, as those who suffered Latin at school may know, *carpe diem* means 'seize the day'. Imagine that you have just arrived home after a shopping trip and are starting to unpack the carrier bags. You discover that a defective plastic bottle has resulted in your freshly baked wholemeal bread becoming marinated in pine-scented cleaning fluid. You can either suffer in silence and do nothing or you can complain and feel better. In

order to take the cathartic route, you must not bury the gripe in the back of your mind and kid yourself that you'll write a letter next week. You won't. Seize the day. Seize the moment. Write a letter without delay.

7. It is worth complaining because there are a large number of companies which, when they get it wrong, will admit that they got it wrong. Some people believe that there is no point in complaining because (a) no one at the organisation gives a damn and (b) a complaint will always be met with nothing more than a polite but dismissive apology. This is not true. Obviously a complaint by me warrants very special attention, but your complaint too will be listened to if the company concerned is reputable and you follow my guidelines. That said, it often surprises even me how seriously some companies take a complaint.

8. Do not fear large and powerful companies or the people who run them. It is a conditioned reflex with most people to believe that letters written on important-looking paper or information generated by computers must be right. Not so. You should believe no one and accept nothing.

9. The mere act of writing a letter gets the complaint off your chest. Complaining purges your soul by dispelling evil spirits which, if left unchecked, will

gnaw away at your mental well-being. By not complaining you store up a guilt complex about what you should have done and you will be reminded at an opportune moment (if your spouse doesn't do it for you) that it really isn't good enough to sit on your backside doing nothing. By taking up the cudgels you take destiny into your own hands. Think of it as vigilantism by correspondence.

10. Swearing is fruitless. Whether you complain on the spot or in writing (I strongly advocate the latter), expletives should always be avoided. Swearing is indulged in by witless whingers whose brawn tends to far outstrip the capacity of their brains. It is quite wrong to assume that an employee of Marks & Spencer or Dixons will respond better just because the account of your grievance has been embroidered with colourful references to the human anatomy. A stream of invective will generally produce the very opposite of a positive reply. The cunning complainer prefers to express his or her complaint by using plain but essentially polite language.

11. When formulating your complaint, do not worry about your legal rights. A wealth of consumer protection legislation exists in this country for the benefit of anyone buying goods and services. Big companies are only too aware of these laws,

whereas the detail, at least, remains a mystery to most consumers. There is no reason to worry about this. If something is wrong, common sense will tell you that it is wrong. There is no reason to not complain just because you are unsure about your legal rights. On the contrary, you will often find that reputable companies will compensate you to an extent which far outstrips the legal obligation to do so. Why? Because they value loyal customers and are constantly striving to improve the quality of their products.

12. A beautifully clear, typed and well-presented letter of complaint is infinitely preferable to a shabby, handwritten one. If you have access to a word processor, these wonderful machines really can give your letters a cutting edge. Typed or handwritten correspondence (especially if the latter is illegible) is often taken less seriously For those of you lucky enough to enjoy the services of a charming and sympathetic secretary, ask very nicely for his or her help and you may get some useful guidance in achieving a really professional touch to your masterpiece. According to my secretary, the going rate for assistance of this kind is a chilled Kit-Kat or a Creme Egg.

13. No institution is too big or too important to receive a letter of complaint. Many people might regard the Post Office, for example, as an

impenetrable fortress, impervious to the wishes of its customers. But behind the grey corporate façade lurks a human being with human emotions and concerns. Governmental bodies and multinational companies might appear to be unfathomable, rigid bureaucracies incapable of responding properly to a complaint. Again, this is not necessarily so. This is a free country and for the price of a first-class stamp you can write to whomever you like. Fear nobody.

14. Don't get personal. When you complain, the source of your dissatisfaction may very often not be the fault of the staff with whom you actually deal. It is fruitless and unfair to vent your spleen on an employee who may well be trying to help you in the face of adversity. Moreover, you could well shoot yourself in the foot by being just plain nasty. Gun for the company if it is this (rather than particular individuals) which has caused you grief.

15. For a letter of complaint, any kind of paper is better than none, but for clarity nothing beats a word-processed page of good-quality white A4. You should regard a single sheet as an ideal target for the length of your masterpiece – brevity is beautiful. Try not to use pages and pages of A5. A Basildon Bond pad is fine for thank-you letters to your grandma but less impressive if you're writing to the Chairman of a multinational business empire.

Obviously, scruffy paper or stuff torn out of an exercise book makes your complaint look offhand and therefore less serious. There is definitely mileage to be had out of a clear, concise, well-laid-out letter. It's a bit like a job interview: appearance should not count for much but in truth it most certainly does.

16. Keep a sense of perspective. A good complainer always remains cool and calm, whatever the circumstances. It may be that your car has broken down for the ninth time, your washing machine is on the blink and you've just had a rotten holiday. But what should you do if you are so angry that you can't even compose a letter? My advice is to forget your woes for a few hours. Think of sunshine and fresh air and go for a walk in the countryside or your local park. After a healthy stroll amid the greenery you will feel 100 per cent better placed to fight your battle. Moreover, you will approach the problem with an infinitely improved perspective.

17. Whenever you write a letter of complaint, always keep a copy. You will need this as a reminder to yourself of precisely what happened and when (especially if the facts are complicated) and as a record of the date on which you first registered your dissatisfaction in writing. If you do not have ready access to a photocopier, a multitude of places,

including libraries and newsagents, will make a copy for a few pence.

18. Prevention is better than cure. It is always advisable to buy goods and services from reputable companies. For starters, you are less likely to encounter a problem worthy of complaint, whereas cowboys invariably mean trouble. Furthermore, if something does go wrong, you are far more likely to obtain a decent response from a company with a good reputation to protect. Good companies not only care about their reputation, but positively want to retain their most loyal customers.

19. You don't get owt for nowt. The world is full of people who have had a dreadful experience with a timeshare company. Although there are several reputable firms selling timeshares, far too many indulge in high-pressure salesmanship of the worst kind. The 'come-on' may involve the promise of a free holiday, a free television set or perhaps free jewellery. The freebie invariably disappoints and is only gained at the price of listening to a three-hour lecture on the joys of timeshare. Do not be lured by fool's gold into believing that timeshare companies are registered charities with altruistic motives. They most certainly are not.

20. Sometimes it is worth using what I call the scattergun method. Instead of writing one letter of

complaint to the Managing Director, I will send exactly the same letter to the Chairman and one other main-board director as well. I don't reveal this fact to any of them. The benefit of this approach is twofold. First, you increase your chances of finding an interested director by 300 per cent. Secondly, even if the three work out what has happened and pass the buck to Customer Services, the complaint will definitely be taken *very* seriously. On one occasion I complained to three directors of a large electrical retailer about a defective hi-fi. The first told me that he could not assist. The second offered a 10 per cent discount on my next purchase. The third offered a full refund. I took the third option.

21. All but the most naïve consumer know the Eleventh Commandment: 'The large print giveth but the small print taketh away.' Always be very careful to check the small print when buying goods or services. A few minutes spent reading it can save months of agony afterwards, particularly if you are spending a large sum of money. The small print will often be found on the back of any documentation which you may be required to sign and will appear under the heading 'Terms and Conditions' or 'Conditions of Sale'. Fortunately, more reputable companies will often use plain English, and you should not necessarily assume that the small print is incomprehensible even

though it is invariably extremely boring. Which companies generate more small print than is good for you? Be especially wary of insurance policies (of all kinds), holidays, mobile-phone contracts, financial or investment contracts (of all kinds) and leasing agreements.

22. The best reason for complaining is that complaining is good for you. In an average week we are all bombarded by a multitude of minor irritants. Those who complain well deal with the problems and feel better for having done so. Those who do not know how to complain bottle up their anger and become embittered. This ineffectual approach to the world is unfortunate because it ignores the fact that complaining is a cathartic exercise – it releases what would otherwise be pent-up frustration. Incidentally, there is a limit. Complaining too much is probably bad for you. I'm trying to cut down to ten a day.

23. If it sounds too good to be true, it *is* too good to be true. Readers of some magazines must be on hallucinogenic drugs if they believe some of the small adverts. 'For a mere £5 you too can become the proud owner of a pair of X-ray glasses.' 'Here's £10, please rush me my copy of *How to Become a Two Hundred Pound Muscleman*.' What do the creators of these products take the public for? The answer is (a) a bunch of fools and (b) a lot of money.

Unfortunately, too many consumers suffer from insatiable greed and really believe that it is possible to get something valuable for nothing. This is not true and rubbish is always best avoided. If you buy a product from a reputable company it might still be rubbish but at least you then have a comeback when you complain.

24. There are some occasions when you have no choice but to complain on the spot. My general advice is that when you encounter a problem it is always far better to write a letter to the person at the top of the company. By doing this you communicate with the person in power and you do so calmly and with clarity. Sometimes this won't work. If your row is with a small local shop or a restaurant which is not part of a large chain, you need to make your point there and then. If you don't you will lose the opportunity to stake your claim to a replacement light fitting or a complimentary bottle of champagne. The basic rules of letter writing still apply: attempt to speak to the organ-grinder rather than the monkey; be firm and assertive but polite; never become abusive; do not indulge in a rant.

25. As obvious as it may seem, if you've got problems with a product you should read the instructions before dashing off a letter of complaint. There is a growing tendency for consumers to shoot from the

hip as soon as something goes wrong. You've just bought a palmtop computer and it doesn't work. You swear at your spouse, you curse the retailer and you immediately start penning an aggressive letter to the Chairman of the company. You assume that your expensive and delicate piece of kit is duff and you vow never to buy a gadget again. Just as you begin to froth at the mouth your calm and level-headed partner points out to you that, if you'd bothered to read page three of the manual, you would have discovered that the small red knob on the side of the machine is the 'on' button.

26. Sometimes there is no one to whom you can complain. Last year a huge, hairy black spider decided to take an evening stroll down my wife's side of the bed just as she was dropping off to sleep. Arachnophobia took an instant grip, and she shrieked and frantically scrambled out of bed. I jumped up too and my size-eleven foot landed on my wife's size four with a crunch. With what she later described as remarkable accuracy, I had managed to dislocate and break her toe. My wife wrongly blames me. I blame the spider. Unfortunately, however, without the spider's address or fax number, even I was powerless to complain.

27. Was the Millennium Bug ever a problem? Having triumphed before with a wasps' nest in my garden

shed, woodworm in my attic and fleas on my cat, I feel more than qualified to make the following suggestions if you are still worried: (1) Sprinkle copious quantities of ant powder around any item in your house containing a microchip (this may include your deep-fry chip pan). (2) If advised by your GP, spray your spouse and children with industrial-strength fly killer. (3) Swap your supersexy high-spec laptop for a pen and a pad of paper. (4) Go to Heathrow, fly to Patagonia, find a cave, become a hermit and stop worrying.

28. Complaining is like a board game. The object of the game is to formulate a simple strategy, apply it and win. If an aggressive style of letter is called for, use that. If flattery or charm will assist you to achieve your aim, employ these as your weapons. If you become embroiled in protracted correspondence, treat it as a fascinating war of attrition. You'll know that your technique is improving when you start to enjoy the game as an end in itself. The trick is to always look at the big picture and concentrate on winning the war rather than the minor skirmishes. The loss of a pawn or two is irrelevant — it's checkmate that counts.

29. Think big. Think small. Children have the same right to complain as you do. Last year I found myself at Heathrow Airport looking after the mountain of luggage that inevitably accompanies a family

holiday. I asked my eldest daughter, Nina (then aged eight), to go to the nearby Costa coffee bar and buy a large espresso for her caffeine-addicted father. Being shorter than the aggressive adults in the queue, she found it impossible to reach the front. Worse, the attendant continually ignored her on the basis that she was an irrelevant child. Nina returned empty-handed and in tears and still recalls the incident. She will probably still remember it in ten years' time, when doubtless she will take her custom elsewhere.

30. What's in a name? In the olden days people with a consumer problem and an ability to put pen to paper would often finish their letter of complaint with the following words: 'If you don't sort this out, I'll write to Esther Rantzen.' Now that dear Esther has moved on to greater philosophical challenges, should consumers threaten the powers that be with my much-maligned name? As far as I am concerned, the answer is yes. Never underestimate the power of the media. If the mere threat of 'being Jaspered' inspires a particular company to take action where otherwise it might not, feel free to add my name to the arsenal of weapons at your disposal. If it works, feel equally free to send me a chunky Kit-Kat as my commission. By the way, if you happen to work in the media or for a law firm, don't be tempted to use the company's headed stationery without authority.

31. Buying by credit card gives you added protection if things go wrong. Many credit-card companies give you free (but limited) insurance covering accidental damage to goods bought with their piece of plastic. There is, however, a far more important reason for using your credit card whenever possible. Under Section 75 of the Consumer Credit Act 1974 you can make a claim for shoddy goods (or goods sold on the strength of a lie) against either the seller or against the credit-card company. If you buy a faulty cooker, for example, and the electrical shop goes bust, register your complaint with the credit-card company. It is supposed to cough up provided the goods cost between £100 and £30,000. Do note that the same protection does not apply to goods purchased with charge cards (like American Express). The credit-card companies hate Section 75, so your claim may well meet with some resistance. Follow the usual Jasper principles and you will eventually triumph.

32. The Complaints Department is never called the Complaints Department. Do not be fooled. Things go wrong and large companies employ teams of people to soothe and pacify aggrieved customers. Unfortunately, very few companies are brave enough to admit openly that they receive complaints. The terms 'Customer Services Department' or 'Customer Relations Department'

are misnomers. These are nothing more than transparent labels that mask the grim truth. These departments deal with complaints. Wouldn't it be refreshing if just one company were honest enough to come clean and describe its Complaints Department by its correct name?

33. Never underestimate the power of love. When writing a letter of complaint you should always address it by name to a person in senior management – the Managing Director or Chairman are both ideal. If you mark the envelope 'strictly private and confidential' it is more likely to reach its intended target, but what if you really want to make sure? One tactic that I have employed in the past is to soak the envelope in perfume (for a male) or aftershave (for a female), seal it with a red heart-shaped sticker and mark it 'S.W.A.L.K.' This approach ensures that the Chairman's secretary is too embarrassed to open the letter and actually gives it to the boss. Ordinarily such letters are passed to the Customer Services Department without senior management becoming involved.

34. Like a beautifully written short story, a well-written letter of complaint should have a clear structure. It should have a distinct beginning, middle and end. The beginning should summarise the problem; the middle should provide the detail; and the end

should be a demand for a remedy. As I said before, even if your story is a long catalogue of disaster, your letter must be concise and punchy. Instead of describing in great detail the different dates, times and circumstances in which, for example, the kitchen fitters failed to turn up or came with the wrong door, tap or whatever, summarise this and simply say the fitters let you down on twenty different occasions – full stop. This will have more impact than a tiresome chronology. Similarly, padding out your letter with other misfortunes to try to gain the reader's sympathy is not relevant or effective – your hip replacement has got nothing to do with your faulty satellite dish. If you keep your letter in shape, you won't lose the plot in the course of writing it.

35. Cheap is expensive. There is something of the skinflint in nearly all of us. We see a special offer at the supermarket and end up buying three monster jars of peanut butter that we don't need. Worse, we might be lured by the gaudy fascia of a foreign discount supermarket. We enter. We buy a monster jar of very cheap peanut butter made in Korea (4000 miles from the nearest peanut plantation). It tastes disgusting. It would have been better to buy an edible brand. The same principle applies to computers, holidays, toys or socks: if you buy something cheap and nasty don't expect perfection.

36. Human beings are sensitive creatures. The tiniest persistent prick from a stray nail in your shoe can be very upsetting. Similarly, if you have spent thirty pence on a packet of crisps only to discover that your beloved snack is home to a cockroach, your sense of indignation can be immense. Once you have realised that the best way to deal with such minor irritations is to (a) treat them as marvellous complaining opportunities (b) enjoy them and (c) do something about them, life suddenly becomes much more bearable. There is nothing so small that it is not worthy of a complaint. If it makes you feel better, get the problem off your chest. If you complain with humour you gain the moral high ground come what may. If you write a light-hearted letter to the cloth-eared old basket of a company chairman (whose capacity to laugh was probably removed long before his dodgy prostate) you win in any event. If you're lucky, he (or she) may allow the scales to fall from his (or her) eyes and respond favourably. In such cases your gripe about a packet of iffy gingernut biscuits will result in a profuse apology and a sackful of the company's finest. If, however, the miserable old devil habitually adopts a Scrooge-like approach to customer care you can still content yourself with the thought that you tried. It is better to have complained and lost than never to have complained at all.

37. Keep the evidence. You do not need me, Miss Marple or Inspector Morse to tell you that evidence is important. If you go on holiday and have a thoroughly rotten time it is an excellent idea to photograph the half-constructed building site next door or the cockroach family sharing your apartment. Why not shoot a video and send that to the Managing Director for him to view at his leisure? Similarly, it is no bad thing to send offending goods to the company concerned – give the Chairman a hot potato and he is more likely to deal with it. In fact, even if your complaint is about a hot potato, why not send the Spud from Hell back to its maker? When I found human hairs in a 'ready meal' once I did precisely that – after photocopying the hairs, of course!

38. Complaining in numbers can bring rewards. If you are one of a number of people with a problem, the collective strength of a group can lend power and credibility to the complaint. The complaint will be taken seriously and a well-drafted joint letter will carry considerable force. On the whole, however, I usually find myself fighting a lone battle. Why? Because most people are too feeble or lazy to stand up for themselves in the face of adversity. By daring to go where others will not, you alone will become the envy of those around you.

39. A good complainer is a humble complainer. If a company performs over and above the call of duty, there is nothing wrong in firing off a letter of compliment. On the contrary, this is an excellent way of raising standards.

14
The Boring Bits

IF IT'S FAULTY AND YOU REALLY WANT TO FACE THE TRAFFIC JAMS, PARKING CHAOS, AND GARGANTUAN CROWDS OF HYSTERICAL PSYCHOTIC MONSTERS, COME BACK TO BRENT CROSS AND WE'LL REFUND YOU!

Kerber

What About the Law?

My general advice is that there is no point in pretending to be a lawyer if you're not one. If you have been hard done by, you know it, the company concerned knows it and no one is remotely interested in what the law has to say. From a customer relations point of view, the law is neither here nor there. Complain if you feel aggrieved. Even if you pursue your claim to the small claims court there is no need for you to spell out the finer points of the latest piece of consumer legislation. Even so, some people feel happier knowing if they are legally correct or not and for that reason I have set out below a few bits of law. You can throw them into your letters of complaint if you think it might add a bit of substance. On the whole it won't. Big companies employ expensive lawyers who don't need to be told what to them is obvious. If anything, your letter may sound a bit pompous. That said, if you like a bit of pomp, here it is:

The Supply of Goods and Services Act 1982

This creates a standard of 'satisfactory' quality. Goods and services must be of 'satisfactory' quality. If they're not, the company concerned is in breach of contract and you can sue. What does 'satisfactory' mean? Well you could pay a lawyer hundreds of pounds to advise you but it varies considerably from case to case. Basically, it is a question of common sense. If you buy a teddy bear and its eye drops out it is not of satisfactory quality. Easy isn't it?

The Unfair Contract Terms Act 1977 and European Directive 1993/13/EC of 15 April 1993 – Unfair Terms in Consumer Contracts as enforced through the Consumer Contracts Regulations 1994 (SI 1994 No. 3159)

See. I told you it was boring. What does this little package of legal gemstones do for you? In short it stops companies inserting silly or oppressive conditions into consumer contracts. For example, if a firework manufacturer puts wording on the side of the firework excluding itself from all liability for personal injury, this will have no effect. If their banger explodes in your hand, the small print won't help them.

The Consumer Protection Act 1987

This one is good. It is the bedrock of consumer safety. If something goes horribly wrong, this Act will generally put the consumer in a strong position. If your washing machine explodes and in the process (a) it blows off your hand and (b) destroys your kitchen, the manufacturers are stuffed. This is a bit like a no-quibble guarantee given by all manufacturers (having had it imposed on them by the law).

The Unsolicited Goods and Services Act 1971

Years ago, companies used to send people things they had never asked for. They then tried to charge them if the goods weren't returned. Amazing but true. If they did it nowadays they would be committing a criminal offence.

The Torts (Interference With Goods) Act 1977

You take your car to the garage to have it serviced. They fail to take good care of it and overnight it is stolen. This Act, amongst other bits of law, is the one to clobber the garage with.

The Trades Description Act 1968

This old favourite is still good law. On the whole it doesn't help you directly but it can be used to put the wind up naughty companies. If a retailer misleads the public by, for example, lying about quality or quantity it commits a criminal offence.

The Misrepresentation Act 1967

This is the Act to rely on if you are dealing with 'porky pies'. If you buy a car on the strength that it can do 50 miles to the gallon, you expect it to do precisely that. If the salesperson deliberately misled you, you can cite the common law of fraudulent mis-representation. If he or she was just stupid or, as the law puts it, 'negligent', then this legislation is designed to help you either get your money back or reject the car completely.

Contract Law Generally

When you buy goods or services, your first port of call should be the company who supplied you the duff slippers or the rotten holiday. You have a contract with them and this generally puts you in a far stronger position than otherwise. You often enter into a contract without really thinking about it – stepping onto a bus or buying a packet of sweets.

The Law of Negligence Generally

Even if you don't have a contract you may have a good claim in law. Before 1932 you had to rely on the law of contract. In that year a famous case created the modern law of negligence. A woman fell sick after drinking a bottle of ginger beer with a snail in it. The House of Lords (our most superior Court) decided that she had a good claim against both the shop that sold her the poisonous brew and the manufacturers. The legal obligations imposed on manufacturers and retailers nowadays are so radically different from 1932 that you are never short of a good case in law if you are well and truly wronged.

The above are just a few juicy snippets of consumer law. If you are really interested in going deeper into the subject you need to buy a more serious book than this.

Conclusion

The Meaning of Life in the Material World

Life in the material world is tough. When you think that the average supermarket sells at least 20,000 different products – to say nothing of department stores, mail order and the Internet – the mind-boggling choice of goods on offer is enough to give you a headache. The slightly hysterical advertisements, the bright primary colours and shrieking special offers all combine to drive a normal human being to distraction. And then things go wrong and you are about to snap. Every week each of us is assaulted by a vast array of niggling mini-disasters. Your credit-card company attempts to overcharge you by £12.34. Your video recorder starts chomping tapes like a starving beaver. Your hamburger tastes like dried sawdust. The only way to avoid going totally mad is to complain.

You are not a prisoner. You have a choice: you can do nothing or you can hit back. The latter course is the best one because if the mini-disasters don't completely wash over you, they eventually affect you like radiation sickness. Little by little they eat away at you. They make you cynical, dissatisfied and ultimately bitter. Complaining is the cure. There is no need to suffer the slings and arrows of outrageous treatment. Powerful companies take your custom for granted and urgently need you to give them a dose of their own medicine. When you do this the medicinal benefit cuts both ways. When a letter of apology arrives, together with a substantial gesture of goodwill, you will feel more than vindicated. You will be cured. What these companies know is that complaining consumers are prone to the effects of the so-called Stockholm Syndrome. In the same paradoxical way that hostages warm to their captors, aggrieved customers can become even more loyal than happy ones. When an offending company remedies the problem and even adds a personal touch, the customer can be won over big time. It's a kind of love-hate thing. Don't be afraid to let Thomas Cook, Sainsbury's or British Gas love you. Don't be afraid to respond to their overtures. Let your feelings be known. Complain.

Useful Addresses

AIRLINES

Aer Lingus
Dublin Airport
Dublin
Ireland
Tel: 353-1-705-2222
www.aerlingus.ie

Air Canada (UK)
Air Canada Complex
Radius Park
Hatton Cross
Feltham
Middlesex TW14 0NJ
Fax: 020-8750-8495
www.aircanada.ca

Air 2000
Commonwealth House
Chicago Avenue
Manchester Airport
Manchester M90 3DP
Tel: 0870-757-2757

British Airways
Waterside
PO Box 365
Harmondsworth
Middlesex
UB7 0GB
Tel: 020-8759-5511
www.british-airways.com

British Midland
Donington Hall
Castle Donington
Derbyshire DE7 2SB
Tel: 01332-854000
www.britishmidland.co.uk

Iberia
27-29 Glasshouse Street
London W1R 6JU
Tel: 020-7413-1297
www.iberia.com

KLM
Endeavour House
Stansted Airport
Essex
CM24 1RS
Tel: 01279-660290
www.klm.uk.com

Lufthansa
World Business Centre
Newall Road
London Heathrow Airport
Hounslow
Middlesex TW6 2RD
Tel: 020-8750-3505
www.lufthansa.co.uk

Qantas
395 King Street
London W6 9NJ
Tel: 020-8846-0466
www.qantas.com.au

Ryanair
Dublin Airport
County Dublin
Ireland
Tel: 00353-1-844-4400
www.ryanair.com

Sabena
Gemini House
2nd Floor, West Block
10/18 Putney Hill
London SW15 6AA
Tel: 020-8780-2270
www.sabena.com

United Airlines
Southside
105 Victoria Street
London SW1E 6QT
Tel: 020-7233-7974
www.ual.com

Virgin Atlantic
Ashdown House
High Street
Crawley
West Sussex RH10 1DQ
Tel: 01293-562345
www.fly.virgin.com/atlantic

BANKS AND BUILDING SOCIETIES

Abbey National
Abbey House
Baker Street
London NW1 6XL
Tel: 020-7612-4000
www.abbeynational.co.uk

Alliance & Leicester
49 Park Lane
London W1Y 4EQ
Tel: 020-7629-6661
www.alliance-leicester.co.uk

Barclays
54 Lombard Street
London EC3P 3AH
Tel: 020-7699-5000
www.barclays.co.uk

Bradford & Bingley
PO Box 88
Crossflats
Bingley
West Yorkshire BD16 2UA
Tel: 01274-555555
www.bradford-bingley.co.uk

Halifax
Trinity Road
Halifax
West Yorkshire HX1 2RG
Tel: 01422-333333
www.halifax.co.uk

HSBC
10 Lower Thames Street
London EC3R 6AE
Tel: 020-7260-0500
www.hsbc.com

Lloyds TSB
71 Lombard Street
London EC3P 3BS
Tel: 020-7626-1500
www.lloydstsb.co.uk

Nat West
41 Lothbury
London EC2P 2BP
Tel: 020-7726-1000
www.natwest.co.uk

Northern Rock
Northern Rock House
Gosworth
Newcastle-upon-Tyne NE3 4PL
Tel: 0191-285-7191
www.northernrock.co.uk

Royal Bank of Scotland
42 St Andrew Square
Edinburgh EH2 2YE
Tel: 0131-556-8555
www.rbs.co.uk

Woolwich
Watling Street
Bexley Heath
Kent DA6 7RR
Tel: 01322-555695
www.woolwich.co.uk

BANKING WATCHDOGS

Office of the Banking Ombudsman
70 Gray's Inn Road
London WC1X 9NB
Tel: 020-7404-9944
www.obo.org.uk

Building Societies Ombudsman
Millbank Tower
Millbank
London SW1P 4XS
Tel: 020-7931-0044

BUILDERS

Anglian
P.O.Box 65 Norwich
Norfolk NR6 9EJ
Tel: 01603-787-000
www.anglianhomes.co.uk

Barratt
Wingrave House
Ponteland Road
Newcastle-upon-Tyne NE5 3DD
Tel: 0191-286-6811
www.ukpg.co.uk/barratt

Bryant Homes
Cranmore House
Cranmore Boulevard
Solihull B90 4SD
Tel: 0121-711-1212
www.bryant.co.uk

Fairclough Homes
Sandiway House
Hartford
Northwich
Cheshire CW8 2YA
Tel: 0161-905-2265

George Wimpey
3 Shortlands
London W6 8EZ
Tel: 020-8748-2000
www.wimpey.co.uk

BUILDING INDUSTRY WATCHDOGS

National House Building Council
Buildmark House
Chiltern Avenue
Amersham
Buckinghamshire HP6 5AP
Tel: 01494-434477

Glass and Glazing Federation
44–48 Borough High Street
London SE1 1XB
Tel: 020-7403-7177

National Inspection Council for Electrical Installation Contracting
Vintage House
37 Albert Embankment
London SE1 7UJ
Tel: 020-7582-7746

Textile Services Association Limited
7 Churchill Court
58 Station Road
North Harrow
Middlesex HA2 7SA
Tel: 020-8863-7755

National Association of Plumbing, Heating and Mechanical Services Contractors (NAPHMSC)
14/15 Ensign House
Ensign Business Centre
Westwood Business Park
Westwood Way
Coventry CV4 8JA
Tel: 01203-470626

Council for Registered Gas Installers
1 Elmwood
Chineham Business Park
Crockford Lane
Basingstoke
Hampshire RG24 8WG
Tel: 01256-372200

CARS

AA
Basingstoke
Hampshire RG21 4XL
Tel: 0890-448-866
www.theaa.co.uk

BMW
Ellesfield Avenue
Bracknell
Berkshire RG12 8TA
Tel: 01344-480-108
www.bmw.com

Daewoo
Daewoo House
Homestead Road
Rickmansworth
Hertfordshire WD3 2LW
Tel: 01923-777-788
www.daewoo.com

Ford
Central Office
Eagle Way
Brentwood
Essex CM15 3BW
Tel: 01277-251-598
www.ford.co.uk

Green Flag
Cote Lane
Pudsey
West Yorkshire LS28 5GF
Tel: 0113-236-3236
www.greenflag.co.uk

Halfords
Icknield Street Drive
Washford West
Redditch
Worcestershire B98 0DE
Tel: 01527-517-601
www.halfords.co.uk

Honda
Highworth Road
South Marston
Swindon
Wiltshire SN3 4TZ
Tel: 01793-831-183
www.honda.co.uk

Jaguar
Brauns Lane
Allesley
Coventry CV5 9DR
Tel: 01203-402-121
www.jaguar.com

Kwik-Fit
17 Corstorphine Road
Edinburgh EH12 6DD
Tel: 0131-337-9200
www.kwik-fit.com

Mercedes-Benz
Mercedes-Benz Centre
Tongwell
Milton Keynes
Buckinghamshire MK15 8BA
Tel: 01908-245-712
www.mercedes-benz.co.uk

Peugeot
Aldermoor Lane
Coventry CV3 1LT
Tel: 01203-884-000
www.peugeot.co.uk

RAC
RAC House
Brockhurst Crescent
Walsall
West Midlands WS5 4QZ
Tel: 0800-731-1104
www.rac.co.uk

Rover
P.O. Box 47
Cowley
Oxford
Oxfordshire OX4 5NL
Tel: 0800-620-820
www.rovercars.com

Vauxhall
Griffon House
Osbourne Road
Luton
Bedfordshire LU1 3YT
Tel: 01582-721122
www.vauxhall.co.uk

Volkswagen
Yeomans Drive
Blakelands
Milton Keynes
Buckinghamshire MK14 5AN
Tel: 01908-679-121
www.vw.co.uk

Volvo
Volvo House
The Parkway
Globe Park
Marlow
Buckinghamshire SL7 1YQ
Tel: 0845-756-4636
www.volvo.co.uk

MOTORING WATCHDOGS

National Conciliation Service
Retail Motor Industry Federation
2nd Floor
Cheshunt House
32 North Street
Rugby CV21 2AH
Tel: 01788-576465

Society of Motor Manufacturers and Traders
Forbes House
Halkin Street
London SW1X 7DS
Tel: 020-7235-7000

GOVERNMENT

Department of Education & Employment
Sanctuary Buildings
Great Smith Street
London SW1P 3BT
Tel: 020-7925-5000
www.dfee.gov.uk

Department of the Environment, Transport & Regions
Eland House
Bressenden Place
London SW1E 5DW
Tel: 020-7890-3000
www.detr.gov.uk

Department of Health
Richmond House
79 Whitehall
London SW1A 2NS
Tel: 020-7210-3000
www.doh.gov.uk

Department of Social Security
Richmond House
79 Whitehall
London SW1A 2NS
Tel: 020-7238-0800
www.dss.gov.uk

Department of Trade & Industry
1 Victoria Street
London SW1H 0ET
Tel: 020-7215-5000
www.dti.gov.uk

Environment Agency
Rivers House
Waterside Drive
Aztec West
Almondsbury
Bristol BS12 4UD
Tel: 01454-624400

Foreign & Commonwealth Office
Downing Street
London SW1A 2AL
Tel: 020-7270-3000
www.fco.gov.uk

Home Office
50 Queen Anne's Gate
London SW1H 9AT
Tel: 020-7273-4000
www.homeoffice.gov.uk

Local Government Ombudsman
21 Queen Anne's Gate
London SW1H 9BU
Tel: 020-7915-3210
www.open.gov.uk/lgo

**Ministry of Agriculture, Fisheries &
Food**
Whitehall Place
London SW1A 2HH
Tel: 020-7238-6000
www.open.gov.uk/maff

Ministry of Defence
Whitehall
London SW1A 2HB
Tel: 020-7218-6645
www.mod.gov.uk

Parliamentary Ombudsman
Church House
Great Smith Street
London SW1P 3BW
Tel: 020-7276-2130
www.ombudsman.co.uk

Post Office
148 Old Street
London EC1Z 9HQ
Tel: 020-7490-2888
www.postoffice.co.uk

Treasury
Parliament Street
London SW1P 3AG
Tel: 020-7270-3000
www.hm.treasury.gov.uk

HOLIDAYS

**Association of Independent Tour
Operators (AITO)**
133a St Margaret's Road
Twickenham
Middlesex TW1 1RG
Tel: 020-8744-9280

**Association of British Travel Agents
(ABTA)**
55-57 Newman Street
London W1P 4AH
Tel: 020-7307-1907

English Tourist Board
Thames Tower
Black's Road
Hammersmith
London W6 9EL
Tel: 020-8563-3367

MEDIA AND ENTERTAINMENT

BBC
Broadcasting House
Portland Place
London W1A 1AA
Tel: 020-7580-4468
www.bbc.co.uk

Carlton
25 Knightsbridge
London SW1X 7RZ
Tel: 020-7663-6363
www.carltontv.co.uk

Granada
Upper Ground
London SE1 9LT
Tel: 020-7620-1620
www.granada.tv.co.uk

Sky
Grant Way
Isleworth
Middlesex TW7 5QD
Tel: 0870-240-4040
www.sky.co.uk

MEDIA AND ENTERTAINMENT WATCHDOGS

Advertising Standards Authority
2–16 Torrington Place
London WC1E 7HW
Tel: 020-7580-5555
Fax: 020-7631-3051
www.asa.org.uk

Radio Authority
Holbrook House
14 Great Queen Street
London WC2B 5DG
Tel: 020-7430-2724

Broadcasting Complaints Commission
Grosvenor Gardens House
7 The Sanctuary
London SW1P 3JS
Tel: 020-7233-0544

Broadcasting Standards Council
7 The Sanctuary
London SW1P 3JS
Tel: 020-7233-0544
www.bsc.org.uk

Press Complaints Commission
1 Salisbury Square
London EC4Y 8AE
Tel: 020-7353-1248

Video Standards Council
Kinetic Business Centre
Borehamwood
Hertfordshire
Tel: 020-8387-4020

RAILWAYS

Eurotunnel
Eurotunnel Shuttle Services
St Martin's Plain
Cheriton
Folkestone
Kent CT19 4QD
Tel: 0990-353-535

Go Ahead Group
Cale Cross House
Pilgrims Street
Newcastle-upon-Tyne NE1 6SW
Tel: 0191-232-3123

Great Eastern
35 Artillery Lane
London E1 7LP
Tel: 0845-950-5000
www.ger.co.uk

Great North Eastern
Station Road
York YO1 6HT
Tel: 0845-722-5333
www.gner.co.uk

Great Western
Milford House MH24
1 Milford Street
Swindon SN1 1HL
Tel: 0870-241-0930
www.great-western-trains.co.uk

London Regional Transport
55 Broadway
London SW1H 0BD
Tel: 020-7918-4300 (buses)
020-7918-4040 (tube)
www.londontransport.co.uk

Railtrack
Railtrack House
Euston Square
London NW1 2EE
Tel: 020-7557-8736
www.railtrack.co.uk

South West Trains
Western House
1 Hobrook Way
Swindon SN1 1BY
Tel: 01793-515-531
www.swtrains.co.uk

Stagecoach Holdings plc
Charlotte House
Charlotte Street
Perth PH1 5LL
Tel: 01738 442111

Virgin
120 Campden Hill Road
London W8 7AR
Tel: 020-7229-1287
www.virgintrains.co.uk

Railway Watchdog
Central Rail Users' Consultative
Committee
Clements House
14 Gresham Street
London EC2Z 7NO
Tel: 020-7505-9090

RESTAURANTS

Beefeater
Whitbread
The Brewery
Chiswell Street
London EC1Y 4SD
Tel: 01580-844-300
www.whitbread.co.uk

Bella Pasta
Whitbread
The Brewery
Chiswell Street
London EC1Y 4SD
Tel: 020-7391-5000
www.whitbread.co.uk

Café Rouge
Whitbread
The Brewery
Chiswell Street
London EC1Y 4SD
Tel: 020-7391-5000
www.whitbread.co.uk

Harry Ramsden's
Larwood House
White Cross
Guiseley
Leeds
West Yorkshire LS20 8LZ
Tel: 01943-879531

Little Chef
Granada Group
Stornoway House
13 Cleveland Row
London SW1A 1GG
Tel: 020-7451-3000
www.little-chef.co.uk

McDonald's
11–59 High Road
East Finchley
London N2 8AW
Tel: 020-8700-7000
www.mcdonalds.com

Pizza Express
363 Fulham Road
London SW10 9TN
Tel: 020-7352-4080

Pizza Hut
Whitbread
The Brewery
Chiswell Street
London EC1Y 4SD
Tel: 020-7606-4455
www.whitbread.co.uk

Planet Hollywood
Trocadero Centre
Coventry Street
London W1
Tel: 020-7287-1000
www.planethollywood.com

Pret a Manger
16 Palace Street
London SW1E 5PT
Tel: 020-7827-8000

Rainforest Cafe
World Headquarters
720 South Fifth Street
Hopkins
MN55343
USA
Tel: 00-1-612-945-5400
www.rainforestcafe.com

TGI Friday
Whitbread
The Brewery
Chiswell Street
London EC1Y 4SD
Tel: 01908-669911
www.whitbread.co.uk

RETAILERS

Allied Carpets
Allied House
76 High Street
Orpington
Kent BR6 0JQ
Tel: 01689-895-600

Ariston (see Merloni)

B&Q
Portswood House
1 Hampshire Corporate Park
Chandlers Ford
Eastleigh
Hampshire SO53 3YX
Tel: 01703-256-256
www.diy.co.uk

Bosch
Grand Union House
Old Wolverton Road
Old Wolverton
Milton Keynes
Buckinghamshire MK12 5PT
Tel: 0870-240-0060
www.bosch-direct.com

Braun
Dolphin Estate
Windmill Road
Sunbury on Thames
Middlesex TW16 7EJ
Tel: 01832-792-000
www.braun.com

Cannon (see General Domestic
Appliances)

Caradon Everest
Everest House
Sopers Road
Cuffley
Potters Bar
Hertfordshire EN6 4SG
Tel: 01707-875-700

Carmen (see Pifco)

Carpetright
Amberley House
New Road
Rainham
Essex RM13 8QN
Tel: 01708-525-522

Comet
Comet House
Three Rivers Court
Rickmansworth
Hertfordshire WD3 2BH
Tel: 01923-710-000
www.comet.co.uk

Courts
Fairlawns
89 Parkside
London SW189 5LR
Tel: 020-8410-9207
www.courts.co.uk

Creda (see General Domestic
Appliances)

Currys
Dixons Group
Maylands Avenue
Hemel Hempstead
Hertfordshire HP2 7TG
Tel: 01442 353000
www.dixons.co.uk

Dixons
Maylands Avenue
Hemel Hempstead
Hertfordshire HP2 7TG
Tel: 01442 353000
www.dixons.co.uk

Electrolux
Oakley Road
Luton
Bedfordshire LU4 9QQ
Tel: 01582-491234
www.electrolux.co.uk

General Domestic Appliances
(Cannon, Hotpoint, Creda)
Grindley Lane
Blyth Bridge
Stoke-on-Trent
Staffordshire ST11 9LJ
Tel: 01733-568989
www.gda.uk.com

Homebase
Beddington House
Wallington
Surrey SM6 0HB
Tel: 020-8784-7200
www.homebase.co.uk

Hoover
Pentrebach
Merthyr Tydfil
Mid Glamorganshire CF48 4TU
Tel: 02685-721-222
www.hoover.co.uk

Hotpoint (see General Domestic
Appliances)

Ideal Standard
P.O. Box 60
Kingston upon Hull
Hull
Humberside HU5 4HS
Tel: 01487-346-461
www.ideal-standard.co.uk

Indesit (see Merloni)

John Lewis
171 Victoria Street
London SW1E 5NN
Tel: 020-7828-1000
www.johnlewis.co.uk

Kenwood
New Lane
Havant
Hampshire PO9 2NH
Tel: 01705-476-000

Magnet
Royd Ings Avenue
Keighley
West Yorkshire BD21 4BY
Tel: 01535-661-133
www.magnet.co.uk

Merloni
(Ariston, Indesit)
Merloni House
3 Cawley Business Park
High Street
Cowley
Uxbridge
Middlesex UB8 2AD
Tel: 01895-858-200

MFI Homeworks
Southon House
333 The Hyde
Edgware Road
Colindale
London NW9 6TD
Tel: 020-8200-8000
www.mfi.co.uk

Moben
Chester Road
Old Trafford
Manchester M16 9HQ
Tel: 0161-872-2422
www.limelight.co.uk

Neff
Appliance Care
Grand Union House
Old Wolverton Road
Wolverton
Milton Keynes
Buckinghamshire MK12 5ZR
Tel: 0990-222-777
www.neff.co.uk

Pifco
(Salton, Tower, Russell Hobbs,
Carmen)
Failsworth
Manchester M35 0HS
Tel: 0161-947-3000

Russell Hobbs (see Pifco)

Salton (see Pifco)

Smeg
Smeg (UK)
87a Milton Park
Abingdon
Oxfordshire OX14 4RY
Tel: 01235-861090
www.smeguk.com

Sony
National Operations Centre
Pipers Way
Thatcham
Berkshire RG19 4LZ
Tel: 0990-111999
www.sony.co.uk

Tower (see Pifco)

Whirlpool
209 Purley Way
Croydon
Surrey CR9 4RY
Tel: 020-8649-5000

Wickes
Wickes House
120-138 Station Road
Harrow
Middlesex HA1 2QB
Tel: 0870-608-9001

Woolworth's
Woolworth House
240/242 Marylebone Road
London NW1 6JL
Tel: 020-7262-1222

RETAIL WATCHDOGS

Mail Order Traders' Association
100 Old Hall Street
Liverpool L3 9TD
Tel: 0151-227-4181

Office of Fair Trading
Field House
Bream's Buildings
London EC4A 1PR
Tel: 020-7242-2858
www.oft.gov.uk

TELECOMMUNICATIONS

British Telecom
81 Newgate Street
London EC1A 7AJ
Tel: 020-7356-5000
www.bt.com

Cable & Wireless
Caxton Way
Watford Business Park
Watford
Hertfordshire WD1 8XH
Tel: 01923-432-000
www.cwcom.co.uk

Ericsson
Telecommunication Centre
Ericsson Way
Burgess Hill
West Sussex RH15 9UB
Tel: 01444-234-567
www.ericsson.com

Orange
St James Court
Great Park Road
Almondsbury Park
Bradley Stoke
Bristol BS12 4QJ
Tel: 01454-624-600
www.orange.co.uk

Vodafone
The Courtyard
2–4 London Road
Newbury
Berkshire RG14 1JX
Tel: 01635-503-915
www.vodafone.co.uk

TELECOMMUNICATIONS WATCHDOGS

**Office of Telecommunications
(OFTEL)**
50 Ludgate Hill
London EC4M 7JJ
Tel: 0845-714-5000
www.oftel.org

UTILITIES

British Gas (Centrica)
Charter Court
50 Windsor Road
Slough
Berkshire SL1 2HA
Tel: 0845-775-4754
www.gas.co.uk

Eastern Group
Wherstead Park
Wherstead
Ipswich
Suffolk IP9 2AQ
Tel: 01473-688-688
www.eastern.co.uk

East Midlands Electricity
P.O. Box 444
Wollaton
Nottinghamshire NG8 1EZ
Tel: 0115-901-0101

London Electricity
Templar House
81–87 High Holborn
London WC1V 96NU
Tel: 020-7242-9050
www.london-electricity.co.uk

North East Water
P.O. Box 10
Allendale Road
Newcastle-upon-Tyne NE6 2SW
Tel: 01912-654-144

North West Water
Dawson House
Great Sankey
Warrington
Cheshire WA5 3LW
Tel: 01925 234000
www.nww.co.uk

Northern Electric
Carliol House
Market Street
Newcastle-upon-Tyne NE1 6NE
Tel: 0191-210-2000

Scottish Power
1 Atlantic Quay
Glasgow G2 8SP
Tel: 01236-729393

Severn Trent Water
2297 Coventry Road
Birmingham B26 3PU
Tel: 0121-722-4000
www.severn-trent.com

South Wales Electricity (SWALEC)
Newport Road
St Mellons
Cardiff CF3 9XW
Tel: 01222-792111

South West Water
Peninsula House
Rydon Lane
Exeter EX2 7HR
Tel: 01392-446-688
www.swwater.co.uk

Southern Electric
Southern Electric House
Westacott Way
Littlewick Green
Maidenhead
Berkshire SL6 3QB
Tel: 01628-822-166

Thames Water
14 Cavendish Place
London W1M 0NU
Tel: 020-7833-6124

Wessex Water
Wessex House
Passage Street
Bristol BS2 0JQ
Tel: 0117-929-0611
www.wessexwater.plc.uk

UTILITIES WATCHDOGS

Director General of Electricity Supply
OFFER Head Office
Hagley House
Hagley Road
Birmingham B16 9QG
Tel: 0121-456-2100
www.open.gov.uk/offer

Gas Consumers Council
Head Office
Abford House
15 Wilton Road
London SW1V 1LT
Tel: 0645-060-708

Office of Water Services (OFWAT)
Centre City Tower
7 Hill Street
Birmingham B5 4UA
Tel: 0121-625-1300
www.open.gov.uk/ofwat

OTHER PROFESSIONAL BODIES AND WATCHDOGS

Accountants (Chartered)

Professional Conduct Department
Institute of Chartered Accountants
in England and Wales
Gloucester House
399 Silbury Boulevard
Central Milton Keynes
Tel: 01908-248100
www.acca.co.uk

Architects

Professional Conduct Office
Royal Institute of British Architects
66 Portland Place
London W1N 4AD
Tel: 020-7580-5533

Auctioneers

Incorporated Society of Valuers and
Auctioneers
3 Cadogan Gate
London SW1X 0AS
Tel: 020-7235-2282

Estate Agents and Surveyors

National Association of Estate
Agents
Arbon House
21 Jury Street
Warwick CV34 4EH
Tel: 01926-496800
www.naea.co.uk

Royal Institution of Chartered
Surveyors (RICS)
12 Great George Street
Parliament Square
London SW1P 3AD
Tel: 020-7222-7000
www.rics.org.uk

Funeral Directors

Funeral Ombudsman
31 Southampton Row
London WC1B 5HJ
Tel: 020-7430-1112

Insurance

**Insurance Brokers Registration
Council**
63 St Mary Axe
London EC3A 8ND
Tel: 020-7621-1061

Insurance Ombudsman Bureau
City Gate One
135 Park Street
London SE1 9EA
Tel: 020-7928-7600

Investments and Finance

Securities and Futures Authority
Cottons Centre
Cottons Lane
London SE1 2QB
Tel: 020-7378-9000

Pensions Ombudsman
6th Floor
11 Belgrave Road
London SW1V 1RB
Tel: 020-7834-9144

Investment Ombudsman
6 Frederick's Place
London EC2R 8BT
Tel: 020-7796-3065

Securities and Investment Board
Gavrelle House
2–14 Bunhill Row
London EC1Y 8RA
Tel: 020-7638-1240

Personal Investment Authority
3rd Floor
Centre Point
103 New Oxford Street
London WC1A 1QH
Tel: 020-7240-3838

Legal

Council for Licensed Conveyances
16 Glebe Road
Chelmsford
Essex CM1 1QG
Tel: 01245-349599

**Office for the Supervision of
Solicitors**
Victoria Court
8 Dormer Place
Leamington Spa
Warwickshire CV32 5AE
Tel: 01926-820082

The Lord Chancellor
The House of Lords
London SW1A 0PW

Legal Services Ombudsman
22 Oxford Court
Oxford Street
Manchester M2 3WQ
Tel: 0161-236-9532

Medical

General Medical Council
178–202 Great Portland Street
London W1N 6JE
Tel: 020-7580-7642

**United Kingdom Central Council for
Nursing**
Midwifery and Health Visiting
(UKCC)
23 Portland Place
London W1N 4JT
Tel: 020-7637-7181

General Dental Council
37 Wimpole Street
London W1M 8DQ
Tel: 020-7486-2171

General Optical Council
41 Harley Street
London W1N 2DJ
Tel: 020-7580-3898

Optical Consumer Complaints
Service
P.O. Box 4685
London SE1 6ZB
Tel: 020-7261-1017

Health Service Ombudsman for
England
Millbank Tower
Millbank
London SW1P 4QP
Tel: 020-7217-4051

Health Service Ombudsman for
Scotland
Ground Floor
1 Atholl Place
Edinburgh EH3 8HP
Tel: 0131-227-465

Health Service Ombudsman for
Wales
Fourth Floor
Pearl Assurance House
Greyfriars Road
Cardiff CF1 3AG
Tel: 01222-394621

Health Service Ombudsman for
Northern Ireland
33 Wellington Place
Belfast BT1 6HN
Tel: 0800-282036

National Lottery

Head of Consumer Affairs
OFLOT
2 Monck Street
London SW1P 2BQ
Tel: 0345-125596

Police

The Police Complaints Authority
10 Great George Street
London SW1P 3AE
Tel: 020-7273-6450

Schools

Independent Appeals Authority for
Schools Examinations
Newcombe House
45 Notting Hill Gate
London W11 3JB
Tel: 020-7229-1234

Tax

Adjudicator's Office
Haymarket House
28 Haymarket
London SW1Y 4SP
Tel: 020-7930-2292

Index